Joseph Herrick:

A Flawed Diamond

Shining for Truth

Martin Wells

© Martin Wells 2018

First published 2018

British Library in Publication Data available

CreateSpace:
ISBN-13: 978-1724260338
ISBN-10: 1724260332

Foreword

Are you familiar with Joseph Herrick? Neither was I until being invited by my fellow church member, Martin Wells, to write this foreword to his new study of this Christian minister. So many of the Lord's faithful servants are largely (or, in some cases, completely) unknown to history. The world does not know them, and often neither does the church. Yet maybe this is how they would wish it, in order that any praise or glory should be rendered alone to the one head of the church, the Lord Jesus Christ, and not be filtered off to them.

Two questions present themselves: who was Joseph Herrick, and why might we be interested in him? The first question is readily answered. He was the evangelical minister of a church in Colchester in the county of Essex. Born in 1794, converted at the age of 16, ordained in 1814, he died in 1865. The author says of him, 'All his life he was a preacher of Whitefield's convictions, declaiming the gospel to all strata of society'. At his ordination, Herrick wrote in his diary, 'I this day give myself up to God and his people'.

As for the second question, the present book provides reasons enough. It gives a harrowing narrative of family sorrows, church problems, doctrinal battles and personal betrayals—as well as a joyful account of gracious conversions, church planting, Christian reconciliations and gospel triumphs. All Christian (and church) life is here. Perhaps above all it is a story of stalwart perseverance through thick and thin—and (more importantly) divine grace given to that end. His prayer when under great discouragement is very moving: 'O Lord, do thou regard thy creature. Suffer me not to be trodden down but deliver me for thy mercies' sake. O, deliver me in thine own way, which is always the best way. Take my troubles from me, or me from them, for Jesus Christ's sake, Amen'. The author describes Herrick's trials as 'character defining and character refining'.

Fundamentally, times do not change. Spiritual battles are ever with us. There are (as in any battle) calmer times, only for hostilities to resume again, and not always when we expect them, or know where they have come from. So, we learn afresh from Herrick our need to fight the good fight of faith and to wage the good warfare, looking to the one who is the Commander of the army of the Lord and the Captain of our salvation.

Early in his life he made a set of spiritual resolutions, pertaining to his devotional life and discipline. Examples are provided in the present book of a number of texts upon which he preached, showing that he was certainly a full-orbed gospel preacher, presenting Christ to sinners and urging upon them the need for repentance and faith—as well as a true feeder of the flock who ministered to them from the entire range of Scripture. It is delightful to read of some of the lives savingly changed by God under his ministry.

The title of this present study, *A Flawed Diamond*, is well chosen. That is what he was—but aren't we all? The truth is—as Joseph Herrick certainly exemplifies—that 'we have this treasure in earthen vessels, that the excellence of the power may be of God and not of us' (2 Corinthians 4:7). And that, surely, is as it should be!

May this book be given a generous reception and be found edifying to all who read it.

Richard Brooks

Preface

'They shall be mine,' says the LORD of hosts, 'on the day that I make them my jewels.' Malachi 3:17

The subject of this biography was perhaps one of the bravest Christians of 19th century England, yet to most people completely unknown. Joseph Herrick became a Congregational minister of a church in Colchester, Essex in 1814, and died after 51 years in office in 1865. Such facts are unsurprising; what is remarkable is the degree of hatred shown towards him, the persecution he endured because of this, and the sheer courage he displayed in being steadfast and immoveable in preaching the truths of the gospel. At the same time there were certain bad traits in his character which spoiled his witness and led to months of depression and later a period of severe chastisement at the Lord's hand. The book is honest about these failings and shows that he was, like us all, a flawed human being, nevertheless loved and disciplined by his Father in heaven and used to God's glory. The trials he went through served to refine his Christian character and make him one of the Lord's jewels, a flawed diamond shining for the truth of the gospel in the darkness of error all around.

This book uncovers the real motives of those who opposed him in his earliest congregation, and their extreme, but finally futile, attempts to eject Herrick and remove the gospel he preached from the building. It required Herrick's extraordinary courage to defend the gospel cause, organise a new building and establish a church from scratch.

The book describes a second, much later, attempt to oust Herrick from his new building by a group of highly political Dissenters. They felt Colchester needed a different sort of Independent church in the town and determined that Herrick's church could be dispensed with and the building used by themselves. This plot was also foiled, and Herrick was sustained to carry on building, with God's aid, a lasting monument to God's grace—a large congregation of saved men and women, standing for the truth of the Bible.

This book seeks to uncover the real Joseph Herrick. You may decide you do not like him, this would be understandable, but would not have caused him a moment's anxiety. It was his standing before his Master in heaven that was his chief concern. A minister who preached at his funeral said: 'of his success, he was content that the Day shall declare it.'

In the UK, we live in days where most people have very little Bible knowledge. The truth of Scripture is opposed by atheistic scientists, ignored, or thought to be irrelevant by the majority, and considered to undermine so-called 'British values' by political leaders. Evangelical Christians can react to this in different ways. This book will challenge those who are tempted to water down 'Christian distinctives' and regard doctrine as divisive and of secondary importance. It will also encourage those at the opposite extreme who are battling to maintain gospel preaching against insuperable odds. Herrick's experience shows us that sheer hard work in sermon preparation, in visiting from house to house, preaching in the pulpit, and above all praying, are still used by God to save souls and add to his church. It still pleases God by the foolishness of preaching to save those who believe. How amazing it is that God still uses frail men and women to accomplish his saving purposes in this world!

A final point emerges from a study of the four books that he wrote. Herrick was a master of close application of scripture to the conscience of his hearers. Gospel preaching to Herrick was not just a careful exegesis of scripture: he applied it and pleaded with his hearers to accept the truth of it and act upon it. He has much to teach us about how to preach the gospel to sinners.

I am very grateful to a number of people who gave me information for this book. Margaret Dudley (née Herrick), a fellow-member of Welcome Hall Evangelical Church, Bromsgrove, is especially to be thanked. She first lent me Herrick's fascinating diary and set me on the path of discovery. Margaret's niece, Julie Herrick, also helped to track down another descendant of the reverend gentleman—Tina Salmon—and point out some of the books Joseph had written. Tina kindly dug out a treasure trove of poetry, prose, letters, the Church Minute Book from the period 1796 to 1816, and even a memento ring belonging to Joseph. I would also like to thank the staff of the Essex Record Office in Chelmsford, Colchester Borough Library and Dr Williams's Library in London, who were unfailingly helpful in making documents available.

I would especially like to thank my son Mike in Pontesbury, Shropshire, and my daughter-in-law Lucy in New York, for the trouble they took in reading the text and offering so many helpful suggestions, pointing out necessary alterations and additions, as well as correcting wrong-headed thinking. I would also like to express my appreciation to Richard Brooks, a fellow church member, who so kindly wrote a foreword to my little work. My final thanks go to my wife Anne for putting up with my four-year obsession, helping on the many trips to Colchester and district and encouraging the writing.

It only remains to pray to the God of the harvest, that he would use this little book to the salvation of poor sinners, and the encouragement of his believing people.

TABLE OF CONTENTS

Chapter 1
The defining incident

The day is Monday June 3rd; the year is 1816. It is only nine o'clock in the morning in Colchester, England, but already the centre of the town is abuzz with rumours. Something highly odd is going on at the Old Meeting Room in Helens Lane. Mrs Lester calls to tell the minister and his wife, "there's some workmen on the roof of the chapel; they're taking the tiles off!" The minister sends up an instant prayer:

O Lord, preserve my mind calm. Prepare me for every event and sanctify unto me whatever occurs.

At 10 o'clock the minister plucks up courage and visits Helens Lane. Sure enough, there's now a large hole in the roof. It appears to him that the tiles are not being carefully *removed*, rather they are being ripped off and thrown into the pews below. The men have been sent under pretence of repairing the building:[1] now it seems clear what they intend to do. By the 5th June they have beaten 'the whole of the roof into the place. Not a tile, a bit of lath or ceiling but what is dismantled and lies in the pews and galleries of the place.'[2] But perhaps the building *did* need a new roof? Two days later, the minister checks with one of his friends, a surveyor. His opinion is clear:

I would defy Colchester to produce a better roof, and I would have engaged to keep it in repair 20 years for £5 per annum.

Now, though, the room is unusable, and the preaching is over.

How could professing church members resort to such violent

measures? What sort of minister could be treated in such a fashion? How did he and the members respond to such treatment?

What was going on in Colchester seems to have been a microcosm of the religious and social turmoil boiling up in England at that time, especially among 'Dissenting congregations' as they were known. This book sets out to trace the life and fascinating career of a highly effective Christian minister of the time. In order to provide a back drop to many of the events of his life and make sense of them we will also outline the history of the Dissenters up to this time.

This crisis, occurring so early in his Christian experience, became the defining moment of his life. It made him wary of shallow Christian profession: only something deeply rooted in Christ could be the real thing. It moulded his church ministry: it would always be Trinitarian, gospel rooted and utterly Biblical. It shaped his personality too: a highly sociable man, he became more cautious, especially in forming Christian relationships. It also made him subject to an irritable temper, a trait which saddened him and led to many penitential comments in his diary in later years.[3] On the positive side, the trial refined the Christian character of someone who became an unusually brave soldier of the cross in early 19th Century Essex. Satan was very active in Colchester 200 years ago; he is equally active today; but we cling like he did to that promise of the great Head of the Church, 'the gates of hell shall not prevail against it!' In spite of many trials, time and again he broke into that marvellous refrain from Psalm 103, 'Bless the LORD, O my soul, and forget not all his benefits.' He could agree with the words of John Newton's well-known hymn, 'Amazing grace':

The defining incident

Through many dangers, toils and snares
I have already come;
'Tis grace has brought me safe thus far,
And grace will lead me home.

Chapter 2
Herrick's early life before his engagement at Colchester

Birth, family and conversion

Joseph Herrick was born in Wolverhampton on 28th March 1794, the second of six surviving siblings given to Joseph and Ann Herrick who were in the jewellery trade in that town. Little is known of Joseph's early life. One obituary mentions 'that Mr. Herrick has left behind him the materials for a memoir, and it is asserted a written life.'[4] Sadly, very little of this has survived. We can piece together information from three documents in the possession of the family. Firstly, there is a hand-written book entitled 'Poetic and Prosaic Sketches,' the largest part of which is dated from October 2–6th 1812. Secondly, there are hand-written diaries covering the years from 1813 to 1819 and 1858. Thirdly, the family, surprisingly, has the Helens Lane Old Meeting House minute book covering the years 1796–1816. His church life from 1816 to 1865 is meticulously recorded, in his own hand, in the Stockwell Church minute book, while comments in the local press, and in the obituary in the Congregational Year Book for 1866, add extra details.

The branch of the Herrick family to which Joseph belonged has been traced back to his great-great grandfather William who was born in 1689 in the very same Wolverhampton parish of St Peters. The jewellery trade in Wolverhampton specialised in striking pieces made from steel, as shown overleaf.[5]

Figure 1: Metallic jewellery made In Wolverhampton[6]

Herrick recalls a little of his childhood in Wolverhampton. He speaks of moving from the darkness of his first home:[7]

To one less dark where I was put to school,
To learn the way to virtue and to God.

Here firmly fixed with earthly comforts blessed
Contentment sweet upon our dwelling smiled.
Each parent now with heartfelt joy caressed,
And fondly wished the welfare of their child.

Sadly, this happy state of affairs was interrupted by grinding poverty.[8]

The wintry blast of indigence so keen
Now blew aloud in our defenceless ears.
No friend appeared from rude insult to screen,
Or wipe away a tender parent's tears.

The problem for the Herrick family was almost certainly the state of their chosen trade in the town.[9]

By the end of the 18th century … cheaper and quicker methods for making this type of steel jewellery had been devised, especially at Boulton and Watt's Soho Works in Birmingham.

This probably explains why the Herrick family moved from Wolverhampton to settle eventually in Clerkenwell London, where more lucrative work in jewellery made from precious metals and stones was available. So, elder sister Sarah was taken with Joseph to live in London some time before the turn of the century. This is where the next sibling Elizabeth was born and registered in Westminster in 1800, while William, Henry and finally John were registered in the Clerkenwell parish in 1802, 1806 and 1811.

There was no relief from penury in London for several years after the move, but God graciously provided work for his father in the jewellery trade and Herrick could take up his education again:[10]

I now resumed what I before began,
First by a mistress then a master's care,
To learn my duty both to God and man,
And guard my youthful mind from ev'ry snare.

It is not certain which school Herrick attended, but his later writings reveal excellent grammar, faultless spelling and a very wide knowledge of poetry and prose. He must have been very well taught, especially as he retained throughout his life an insatiable desire for knowledge.

The attractions of London were irresistible to the young Herrick, and he left school at 14. He speaks of his interest in the stage and the moral danger in which he became embroiled:[11]

Of all the ills, which London youths surround,
The stage attracted my attention first.

My passion soon increased for public plays,
And to the depth of folly soon I sunk.
What now employed the leisure of my days
Was cursing, swearing, gaming, getting drunk.

Despite the downward spiral Herrick was in, he had serious thoughts of making a career of the stage, especially as he had a gift for public speaking. All this was going on while he was apprenticed to John Douglas, a Silversmith in Red Lion Street, Clerkenwell.[12]

God intervened in a remarkable way when he was wonderfully converted at the age of 16. The circumstances of this have striking parallels to the conversion of Charles Spurgeon many years later.[13] On a Sunday in his seventeenth year he was going for a walk in the area round Clerkenwell. He was just passing Spa Fields Chapel when a heavy shower came on and having no umbrella he sought shelter within the chapel. Spa Fields Chapel was part of Lady Huntingdon's Connexion[14] and was well-known as a large Dissenting chapel where the gospel was regularly preached. The challenge of the gospel brought him into intense conflict of soul.[15]

'Is there a God?' with eagerness I cried.
'If so I'm lost, is there a Hell? No, no!'
To drown the thought in vain I ofttimes tried,
But conscience followed like a dauntless foe.

The contest went on for many days, but God brought him through:

As liberty to one in chains long bound,
Or as cold water to a thirsty soul,
Just so with me the Gospel's joyful sound,
By faith refreshed restored and made me whole

With joy he could confess that he was 'snatched as a brand from the burning,' and was 'made wise unto salvation.'[16]

Perhaps the best commentary on this life changing event comes in one of the hymns Herrick compiled for his congregation in the 1830s:[17]

1. How precious art Thou dear Redeemer to me:
What wonderful beauties in Thee do I see!
Thou'rt all that I want and Thy voice or Thy sight
Give rise in my heart to the purest delight.

2. I think on past seasons with sorrow and shame,
(I loved not Thy person, nor joyed at Thy name,)
When sin bound my heart and my eyes with a spell,
And Satan was leading me blindfold to hell.

3. 'Twas then, dearest Saviour, Thy word reached my ears;
Thy form struck my eyes, and o'erflowed them with tears;

My conscience was pained, and my soul was surprised
That I had so lovely a Saviour despised.

4. From that melting moment my heart was Thine own,
And felt that Thy love had so made it Thy throne;
That all its affections moved but at Thy word—
Its Lover, its Saviour, its Friend, and its Lord.

5. Since then, ah! How oft have I wandered from Thee;
But still Thou art precious and faithful to me;
I grieve Thee, yet proofs of Thy love I receive,
And find Thee more precious, the more I believe.

Church member and fledgling preacher

After that 'melting moment,' Herrick sought out a good church
where his soul could be fed from the Scriptures, and where he
could join with other believers in praising his precious Saviour.
He became a member of City Chapel, Grub Street, where the
pastor was Charles Buck. Buck was a great help to Herrick. He
himself had been converted in his early teens and had started
preaching at the age of 18.[18] Herrick had fond memories of this
man, calling him 'my dear pastor,' and writing in his diary:

> I knew him but a short time, but I love him much. His
> memoirs and letters are interesting, and well develop his
> real worth. They show the power of his mind and the
> excellent qualities of his heart.

Herrick began as a Sunday School teacher, and then as Buck
saw his gift developing he encouraged him to train for the
ministry. Hoxton Academy was the place of choice for
Dissenters from the Independents (Congregationalists), but in
1813 there were no places available at that excellent
establishment. Thomas Wilson, the great philanthropist among

the Independents, took Herrick under his wing and suggested he should go instead to John Thornton in Billericay, Essex. Thornton had been pastor of Billericay Congregational Church since 1800 and had recently started his own academy to mentor students whose personal circumstances debarred them from joining larger Christian colleges.[19]

So it was, that Herrick began as a preacher under John Thornton's tutorship. He left home on the day after his 19th birthday, 29th March 1813. He preached in Independent churches, little or large, roughly within a 10-mile radius of Billericay, returning to his base at Thornton's each night. Herrick was a model of hard work during the six months he was at Billericay, preaching 62 sermons in exactly six months, and at 11 different locations. He was always grateful for John Thornton's mentoring at this point in his life and referred to him more than once as 'my kind friend Mr Thornton,' visiting him often and writing for help and advice during his early years at Colchester.

Remembering God's hand upon him

Old Testament believers were encouraged to remember the day the LORD delivered them from slavery in Egypt:

'Remember this day in which you went out of Egypt, out of the house of bondage; for by strength of hand the LORD brought you out of this place.' Exodus 13:3

The privilege of doing this is felt by New Testament believers too, as they partake of the Lord's Supper and remember all he suffered to deliver them. Herrick could never forget God's amazing grace. As a jeweller's apprentice, Herrick was determined to make a special memento. He had a ring made, which is still in the family's possession more than 200 years later. His initials, and the two special dates to remember are shown in the photographs below:

Figure 2: JH Initials on Herrick's memento ring

October 2, 1810 is a Tuesday. This is almost certainly the date of his conversion. It is in his 17th year and agrees with the information given in his obituary in The Congregational Year Book of 1866.

Figure 3: Oct 2, 1810 date on Herrick's memento ring

Figure 4: Oct 6, 1811 date on Herrick's memento ring

The 1811 date is a Sunday, and, I suggest, refers to the beginning of his service for the Lord in a public capacity, presumably in his local church.

The ring was probably not intended for wearing. The

inscriptions are still remarkably crisp after all this time. He kept it, I venture to say, as a precious memento of the Lord's goodness to him.

The seriousness with which he took his entry into Christian service is clear from some lines he wrote round about this time:[20]

Lord teach Thy youthful servant how to pray,
Who feels his strength unequal to his day.
O grant me this important thing I ask:
O fit me for the sweet but awful task.
Thou knowest my desire is to do good
By setting forth the power of Jesu's blood;
To justify Thy wondrous ways with men;
To teach them that they must be born again.
To tell them of a Saviour's wondrous love,
And guide their feet to realms of bliss above;
To lure poor sinners by the gospel's charms;
Portray a Saviour with extended arms.

Fledgling preacher on supply at Grays

Around August 1813, Herrick preached for the first time at a town called Grays some 15 miles to the south of Billericay, on the north bank of the Thames. Fourteen of his last 20 preaching engagements while under Thornton's tutelage were at Grays, so it would have been no surprise when the church asked him to stay on a more regular basis as supply, until they were clear how to proceed. September 29, 1813 was the day Herrick started in this new way, and it was the day he began his diary. The seriousness with which he regarded this new staging post in his Christian life can be judged from his first entry:

On this day my engagement commenced at Grays. An important change has now taken place in my station, an innumerable host of difficulties press upon me, but I have made up my mind to meet such. I surrender myself to the Lord, I beg of him to support me, to protect me and make me useful. Lord grant me a clear head, a devout heart, and a strong constitution. May I burn with zeal for thy glory, may I have many souls to my hire, may an house be created here for thee, and may it be filled with thy glory, Amen.

It appears that the church at Grays had asked him to preach four times each week: Sunday afternoon and evening with Monday and Wednesday evenings as well. To modern Christians this sounds like a heavy work load, but it was by no means unusual. In fact, it was missing one vital ingredient, probably the key meeting of the week: the Sunday morning meeting! It appears that the appointment was *only part time*. He was not involved in any of the important decisions of church life made at the monthly church meeting, neither was he expected to do any pastoral work. A very outgoing young man was in effect being asked to act as a supply preacher only. Without complaint, Herrick threw himself into the appointment with enthusiasm. The meetings were very well attended most of the time, the exceptions being when the weather was poor in the late autumn months. Church members commented favourably on his preaching, but his make-up was such that he found it very hard to live with so little social interaction. As an earnest Christian he filled his time usefully, devouring Christian literature, filling his mind with the Scriptures. One day he fell ill:

Very unwell, spit a little blood in the morning, attended my school, read nothing all day but a few meditations in 'the Christian oratory' on grace, several of them very excellent. Expounded in the evening at Grays. Pain in my stomach came on with speaking.

We see that he did not allow illness to get in the way of his service to the Lord. Not once did he fail in his preaching duties; this was a feature right to the end of his days. Herrick seems to have had a very robust constitution and a God-given desire to carry on whatever the odds. But there was a cost: the isolation led to lowness of spirit. He sought advice from Mr Wilson in London; he grew impatient, and depressed when one of his friends was slow to reply.

One particular event seems to have made him decide that Grays could never be his permanent place of ministry. All his life Herrick worried about financial security. This was on his mind at this time because he was engaged to be married, and so needed enough to support a wife and family. In early December he was amazed to discover that a few friends at Purfleet were more generous in giving money than the whole membership at Grays.

If this was the case what financial security would he ever have as a minister at Grays church? This was the straw that broke the camel's back. He wrote to Mr Wilson for advice, then went back home to see him in person in London in mid-December. After visiting many of his friends there, he travelled to see Rev. Samuel Douglas in Chelmsford, his future father in law's brother, and a very godly minister whose advice he often sought. Reading between the lines, it looks as though he learned from Samuel Douglas of the vacancy in Helens Lane in Colchester. They had been without a minister for more than 12 months, the church was reasonably well endowed, and so an introduction to the pulpit was made.

There is another reason Herrick considered towns close to Chelmsford for ministry opportunities. His wife-to-be, Ann

Douglas, had inherited, or was about to inherit, significant property in the village of Springfield, just to the east of Chelmsford. Colchester was the nearest large town to Chelmsford and was sufficiently close to collect the rental income from the cottages there, and so provide a useful supplement to a ministerial salary.[21]

It is easy to pass judgment on Herrick's behaviour 200 years after the event. It does *look* as though he *abandoned* the Grays supply in mid-December, and the church were certainly very cool towards him when he made his position clear in January 1814. On the other hand, surely a church who had seen him in action for 3 months and heard him preach no less than 66 times could have properly ordained him by now! There was clearly very little communication from the leadership at Grays. As far as Helens Lane was concerned, great good actually came from this period at Grays: Herrick laid the foundations of his future Christian ministry in a set of resolutions, made towards the end of his time there:

Hoping that whilst I live I may live to the Lord and be enabled to redeem the time because the days of men are both short and evil, I desire as far as possible to act according to the following Resolutions.

To resolve first to spend about half an hour every morning with God.

Resolution 2: to read devotional books or short sermons from 8 to 10.

Resolution 3: to devote from 10 to 12 to miscellaneous reading, sermonizing etc.

Resolution 4: to pray for divine illumination about 12 & carefully peruse the holy scriptures till about 2 o'clock.

Resolution 5: to read after dinner history, biography etc. till 4.

Resolution 6: to read the best divinity I can from 4 till about 8.

Resolution 7: to read after family worship etc. any miscellaneous pieces which may appear suitable, be careful to maintain conversation in a serious and edifying way.

Resolution 8: to write down every night if possible all I have read during the day where I have preached etc.

Resolution 9: to adhere to this plan as near as possible when I spend the whole day indoors and when I take exercise to take it out of the time for miscellaneous reading.

Resolution 10: to conclude the day with private prayer and not excuse myself with having performed family worship.

Joseph Herrick

November 25 1813

There is abundant evidence that Herrick kept to these splendid godly resolutions all through his ministry, and they explain his exceptional usefulness during his more than half a century in gospel work.

Chapter 3
Dissenting churches up till the early 19th century

The English church from the Reformation to the great ejection of 1662

To understand the church turmoil in early 19th century Colchester we need to go back to the Reformation of the 1500s. God had done an amazing work of transforming lives as the Bible became available in English simple enough even for the ploughboy to understand. The prime architect, under God, of this translation work was that genius of a linguist, William Tyndale. By the early 1600s his work had been crystallised in the King James Version Bible. The King James translators admitted that they never thought:

> to make a new translation, nor yet to make a bad one a good one ... but to make a good one better ...

In code they were referring to Tyndale's translation which scholars reckon constitutes at least 90% of the KJV text.

While lives had been changed through the word of God, church government and worship were far more resistant to reformation. The king of England was the official head of the Church of England; no other type of church was officially permitted. This denomination still had its bewildering, unbiblical hierarchy of archbishops, bishops, vicars, rectors, curates, canons, and so on. Practices such as the wearing of showy vestments, altar use, making the sign of the cross and written prayers, detracted from the pure worship of God. Worse, there was no clear distinction made between believers and unbelievers: anyone from the parish was free to go to church and take part in the Lord's Supper. The idea of the gathered local church as a company of believers saved through faith in the atoning work of Jesus Christ was foreign to many church leaders. These were all practices and attitudes left over from the Roman Catholic era.

The Puritans were the godliest men of that age. They pressed for change, but their protests fell largely on deaf and unregenerate royal ears. In spite of little support, these good men began to set up churches along Biblical lines. There was intense discussion about Biblical doctrine which resulted in the publication of the highly valuable Westminster confession of 1646.

The great ejection of 1662 and the rise of Dissenters

Things changed radically with the return of royalty in the person of King Charles II in 1660. The Commons introduced the Act of Uniformity which required all worship to be carried out according to the Church of England Prayer Book of 1604. A short time later the Corporation act was passed which demanded that Communion be received 'according to the rites of the Church of England.' The demand was in effect to agree with the entire contents of the Prayer Book of 1662. This was an intolerable burden on the conscience of the godliest ministers in the land and an interference with their liberty. The result was that nearly 2000 ministers of the Church of England were ejected from their positions.

Those who refused to conform to the prescribed Church of England worship became known as Nonconformists, or more usually Dissenters. These Christians fell into three main groups:

1. Baptists, 2. Presbyterians 3. Independents or Congregationalists.

The *Baptists* were undoubtedly the oldest of the Dissenting groups. Long before the Great Ejection, many of them had separated themselves from Popery, and later the Church of England, and set up local churches of baptized believers. This noble army of Baptist believers suffered along with their Presbyterian and Independent brothers following the Act of Uniformity.

Our main concern in this book, however, is to trace the fortunes of the Presbyterian and Independent believers, as this has direct relevance to the situation in Colchester in Herrick's day. It was from the 2000 ejected ministers that most of the original churches of these denominations were derived, though, of course, many such churches were added at a later date.

The *Presbyterians* of this period were the closest in belief and practice to the established Church of England. (The English Presbyterians we are discussing here are to be carefully distinguished from the Scottish Presbyterians with their rule by elders and synods and acceptance of the Westminster Confession as a doctrinal standard. The Scottish Presbyterian church was *imported* into England during the 1800s.) English Presbyterian Church government was in the hands of the minister and lay elders, but ministerial appointment and ordination were assisted by ministers from other Presbyterian churches.

The Church of England had divided the land into dioceses, where the Bishop ruled, and smaller parishes within each diocese where the vicar of the local parish church was located. Although Presbyterians were unhappy with the interference of bishops in local church matters, *they were content to stay within a parochial system.* This was the case even though it allowed anyone living in the parish to take communion, regardless of his or her spiritual state. The Presbyterians would seek to guard against scandalous living communicants by church discipline, administered at a local level. To qualify for admission to communion no more was required of the candidate than:[22]

> a credible profession of faith such as a normal person could compass who had been schooled in the catechism.

Independents disapproved of this; they wanted a church to be *a local gathering of saved believers*. Church government was under the local minister/elder and deacons, and people who desired membership were expected to give a credible account of their conversion. This would be read to all believers at a church meeting where members would vote for or against their reception into church fellowship. By this means, it was hoped to protect the church from nominal Christians or bad-living professors. All church disciplinary matters would be dealt with at the church meeting, under the guidance of minister and deacons.

Richard Baxter, who acted as spokesman for Moderate Episcopalians and Presbyterians, was opposed to this Independent way of gathering church members. He told John Owen, the Independent:[23]

> They (the Presbyterians) think ... that your way ... tendeth to extirpate godliness out of the land; by taking a very few that can talk more than the rest, and making them the Church, and shutting out more that are worthy,

Many attempts were made to unite Presbyterians and Independents, but the differences between them were too large: Presbyterians ultimately wanted to be *understood* within the Anglican structure; Independents wished to be *tolerated* as a separate church operating across traditional parish boundaries. Once the Great Ejection had occurred, *understanding* within the Church of England structure became impossible: *toleration* was the best that could be expected.

Moral decline from 1662 to the early 1700s

The act of toleration of 1689, following the arrival of William of Orange as the king of England, saw the start of more comfortable times for those Christians who had been marginalised and persecuted after 1662. We might have expected true Christianity to have flourished in these favourable circumstances: the opposite was in fact the case.

The Restoration of the monarchy in 1662 had opened the floodgates to licentiousness. Unregenerate people threw off the restraints the Puritans had put in place, and Charles II led the way in dissolute behaviour in the royal household.

The moral decline which began in the 1660s became more rapid as the 1700s began. A growing problem in the early 1700s was drunkenness. Gin was virtually unknown in England in the 1600s and was associated anyway with a prohibitive import tax, but it was the favourite drink of William of Orange's soldiers. After William came to the throne it became very popular, especially when the tariff on it was lifted and English distilleries were set up. So cheap was this highly intoxicating spirit that one shop advertised it: 'drunk for a penny, dead drunk for two, clean straw for nothing.' The Gin drinking habit had a devastating effect on English society. Perhaps the worst effect it had was that indicated by Bishop Benson, when, towards the close of his life he stated:[24]

> Gin has made the English people what they never were before—cruel and inhuman.

What England needed was the gospel of Jesus Christ, whose blood can make the foulest clean. The churches of the early 1700s were unready for the task. It took the miracle of the God sent 18th century revival under Whitefield, the Wesley brothers, Rowland and others to turn matters round.

State of Dissenting churches in early 1700s

The Dissenting churches were not in a great shape at this time. The general cynicism had largely sapped their strength. The 18th century is often popularly called the Age of Enlightenment. During this century all scientific and political ideas had to be judged at the bar of reason. It was not long before the Bible itself had to be arraigned there too. The long-accepted belief in the inspiration, infallibility and sufficiency of Scripture began to come under attack. In many pulpits reason was elevated above the Word of God. Mr Barker (1682–1762), minister at Salters Hall, Cannon Street, London, had this to say about the Dissenting churches of his time:[25]

> The Dissenting interest is not like itself: I hardly know it. It used to be famous for faith, holiness, and love. I knew the time when I had no doubt, into whatever place of worship I went among Dissenters, but that my heart would be warmed and comforted, and my edification promoted. Now … one's ears are so dinned with reason, the great law of reason, and the eternal law of reason, that it is enough to put one out of conceit with the chief excellency of our nature, because it is idolized, and even deified.

The moral and spiritual decline which began in the reign of Charles II emboldened a number of writers to spread the poison of unbelief throughout the land. It was during this period that Deism became popular. Deism purports to believe in the existence of a supreme being, God, who does not intervene in the universe. The welcome given to this woeful belief can be traced to two sources. The first was the scientific discoveries of Isaac Newton (1642–1727). This great man's work showed his generation that the universe was not chaotic but held in order by precise mathematical and physical laws. Rather than lead people to worship the great Designer and Creator God, for some:[26]

> God seemed to lose His personal character as He became the Great Mechanic of a Great Machine, the world, and the Great Architect of a great building, the cosmos.

This impersonal God was viewed as having wound up the clock of the universe, and then stood back and let it run of its own accord. How different this from the personal God of the Bible, who so loved the world that he gave His only begotten Son!

Whereas Newton was held to have given a scientific basis to belief, the philosopher John Locke (1632–1704) was very much the architect of the philosophy behind it. Locke was the moving spirit of the eighteenth century and its 'enlightened' understanding. Among many books that he wrote, one which was particularly influential was 'The Reasonableness of Christianity.' Locke was at pains to establish that God may be known purely through reason. This is clear from the quotation below:[27]

> God, out of the infiniteness of his mercy, has dealt with man as a compassionate and tender Father. He gave him reason and with it a law, that cannot be otherwise than what reason should dictate, unless we think that a reasonable creature should have an unreasonable law.

Locke sought to reduce Christianity to the bare minimum,

making faith a mere mental assent to the belief that Christ is the Messiah. In passing, he affirmed that Jesus was *made* Son of God at his birth, rather than being eternally so. Much of what Locke was doing was designed to undermine the creeds and look at the Bible alone. It sounded very good, but it was not very long before belief in the Trinity was under attack, then the atonement of Christ, and the foundation of the inerrancy and sufficiency of Scripture. Decades before, Richard Baxter, who often acted as spokesman for the Presbyterians, had said:[28]

What more can be done to the disgrace and ruin of Christianity than to make the world believe we have no reason for it?

Baxter had also written a book in 1667 entitled, *The reasons of the Christian religion*. Superficially, Locke seemed to be reinforcing the same message, though nothing could have been further from the truth. Baxter was stressing that Divine truth never bypasses the mind; Locke was bringing the truth of scripture to the bar of human reason. For the English Presbyterians, a book from Locke whose title resembled that from their great supporter, was just what they wanted to read. The inevitable happened—young Presbyterian ministers imbibed error and began to preach it. Two very influential works were published during these years of decline: William Whiston's *Primitive Christianity Revived*, 4 volumes, 1711, and Samuel Clarke's *Scripture Doctrine of the Trinity*, 1712.

These titles sounded wholesome but were full of heretical doctrine. They were devoured by some theological students, especially those in English Presbyterian academies.

The Salters Hall watershed in 1719

Matters came to a head for Dissenters in 1719. Some divinity students in the English Presbyterian academy in Exeter had begun a correspondence with William Whiston. Three of them, after their ordination, began in their sermons to avoid any reference to scriptures which might support the Trinity, and omitted to end their services with the Trinitarian benediction. One of these students admitted afterwards:[29]

> While I lived here some of us fell into the Unitarian[30] scheme about the Trinity.

It was not long before orthodox ministers and congregations noticed these things. The upshot was that seven Exeter ministers were summoned by thirteen laymen and asked to subscribe to the first article of the Church of England—relating to the Trinity. This, most of them refused to do, protesting that Scripture alone was their final arbiter. No agreement could be reached.

As things had come to an impasse, both sides sought advice and help from colleagues in London. A general meeting was called for Dissenting ministers from London with special invitations to those from further afield. One hundred and ten men—Baptist, Congregationalist and Presbyterian ministers— met at Salters Hall in London for two days: 19 and 24, February 1719.

You might have thought the discussion would hinge around the dangers of Unitarian belief, its unscriptural character, and how to curb its further advance. However, the main problem all along was that the delegates knew that they would need to send advice to the ministers in Exeter. How would this be done? If it were a form of words to which the ministers had to subscribe, many of the delegates would be unhappy. Less than 60 years before, their godly forebears had been cast out of the established church because they would not subscribe to the form of words in the Prayer Book. How could they now impose another set of words on the ministers in Exeter? The force of this dilemma was felt by godly orthodox ministers as well as those in favour of Unitarianism. Isaac Watts wrote to Cotton Mather in America,[31]

> I confess, if the matter of debate at London was the glorious doctrine of the Trinity ... there would be more just occasion for fervour of spirit ... But ... the subject of the contest in this city is reduced to this one point, viz. which is the best way to preserve truth and peace, whether by subscribing the words of Scripture or human forms ...

After much heated debate, the 110 ministers met on the second day, and it was agreed to take a vote. Those who were against inserting a declaration concerning the Trinity in the advice to Exeter were to go into the gallery. Those who were in favour of a subscription to a form of words would stay downstairs. The division became quite noisy; partisan phrases were bandied about:[32]

> You that are against persecution, come upstairs! Which was pretty evenly balanced by one on the other side, calling out, you that are for the doctrine of the Trinity, stay below!

When order had been restored, and the votes counted, it was found that those who were against advising a subscription to a statement about the Trinity had carried it by 57 votes to 53. An interested onlooker declared: 'The Bible carried it by four.'

The Dissenters were now divided into Subscribers and Non-Subscribers: a lamentable result for church unity. There was a marked difference between the major Dissenting bodies. The Independents (Congregationalists) were strongly in favour of subscription to a form of words, as were the Particular Baptists. Among the English Presbyterians, on the other hand, there was a large majority who wished to follow in the footsteps of

Richard Baxter in preferring a 'Bible only' approach.

Salters Hall had failed to give a clear lead to orthodox belief; it now became open season for all sorts of heretical views to be aired. From that time onwards, many of the Non-Subscribing Presbyterian churches espoused increasingly heretical views, while the majority of Congregational and Particular Baptists largely maintained their doctrinal purity.

Congregationalists and Presbyterians from 1719 to 1819

What happened to Presbyterian and Congregational churches in the 100 years that followed Salter's Hall? The first thing we can be certain of is that numerically, the Presbyterians declined dramatically, while Congregational churches held their own or increased. Statistics are hard to come by, but at the great ejection of 1662, the affiliation of the Dissenting ministers has been estimated as:

Congregationalist   309[33]
Presbyterian   1700[34]

Data of the number of churches from the early 1800s show the contrast:[35]

	1812	1827
Congregationalist	808	1203
Presbyterian	247	
Unitarian		204

Table 1: Dissenting church breakdown in the early 1800s

The fact that Bennett chooses to denote Presbyterian

churches as Unitarian in 1827 tells us everything about the direction these churches went in the 15 years after 1812.

There were two main reasons for the decline of the English Presbyterians.

1. The threat of Unitarianism was not taken seriously enough

Good men among the Dissenters deemed the threat of Deism, particularly from around 1725 onwards, to be worthy of strong opposition. Men like Isaac Watts and Philip Doddridge devoted considerable time to this effect in writing and preaching. Much as these efforts were appreciated at the time, a number of weaknesses are evident in hindsight. Skeats has this to say about the efforts of those who opposed Deism:[36]

> They fell into a habit of treating Christianity as an intellectual creed, a system of morals, and a means of virtue. In no age, probably, have so few appeals to the spiritual affections of men been made as were made during the age of Deism.

Another real problem was that in attacking Deism, good men like Watts and Doddridge were joining hands with anti-Trinitarians, who also objected to this cult. Among their colleagues were Nathaniel Lardner, who questioned the pre-existence of Christ before the Incarnation; Joseph Hallett who denied the Trinity and was one of the causes of the Salters Hall controversy, and William Sherlock, whose defence of the Trinity led him to propound the three persons of the Trinity as three distinct infinite minds—a sort of tritheism.

Neither Watts[37] nor Doddridge[38] were totally clear about the Trinity themselves, perhaps unsurprisingly with this group of colleagues in the camp. In Doddridge's case there was the added complication of having been mentored from a young age by Samuel Clarke who was censored by the Church of England for his work on the subject of the Trinity. Although both these men were devout evangelical Christians, they were a product of their time with its special pressures and ways of thinking. The heresies of Deism were serious, but in tackling them they conceded far too much ground on the equally important matter of the Trinity. In projecting a full-frontal attack against Deism, they were ambushed from behind by the neglected enemy, viz Unitarianism, or, as it was called at the time, Socinianism.[39]

2. Errors were taught at Dissenting academies

The earliest academies had been strictly orthodox, that is Calvinistic, in their theology. By the 1730s however, all the leading academies favoured by English Presbyterians had drifted to more unorthodox views. This was particularly the case with the academies at Taunton, Exeter, Warrington and others in Lancashire. Sadly, however, even Doddridge's Northampton academy was not immune from errors. Doddridge was not entirely orthodox about some aspects of the Trinity. He had studied under John Jennings at the Kibworth academy before he was asked to take it over from his former tutor, which he eventually did at Northampton. The style of Jennings teaching was described by Doddridge in a letter to Samuel Clarke:[40]

> Mr. Jennings encourages the greatest freedom of inquiry, and always inculcates it as a law, that the scriptures are the only genuine standard of faith ... In this course Mr. Jennings does not follow the doctrines or phrases of any particular

party; but is sometimes a Calvinist, sometimes an Arminian, and sometimes a Baxterian, as truth and evidence determine him.

When he was in charge, Doddridge was strict in the way he selected candidates for the academy, expecting a written statement of their faith in their own words. If he was not happy with this, the candidate would not be accepted. His method of teaching, however, was very much along the open and liberal lines adopted by Jennings at Kibworth. Many students relished the atmosphere of free enquiry that permeated the academy, which in Doddridge's lectures was regularly accompanied by a statement of his own decidedly orthodox opinions. Clifford suggests that Doddridge was of the view that 'orthodox Christianity could withstand all the attacks of scepticism and unbelief.'[41] The evidence suggests something different. Doddridge grieved over the number of his students who drifted from gospel truth. One of these was Charles Bulkley (1719–1797), who is of special interest here for two reasons: firstly, because he was the grandson of the saintly Matthew Henry; secondly, because he became one of the first Unitarian ministers at Helens Lane, Colchester (from 1739–1741) and shared in turning that church away from gospel truth.

It is important not to *overstate* the problem of this method of teaching under Doddridge's watch. There were 205 students taught at Northampton over the 28 years Doddridge was the chief tutor there (1723–1750). The records[42] indicate that some 17 students drifted into Arian or Unitarian beliefs, and then preached it from church pulpits. Even one is to be regretted of course, but we can compare this with what happened after Doddridge's death and the academy was moved to Daventry, where the tutors were Caleb Ashworth, later joined by Thomas Belsham. The Daventry academy (1752–1789) trained 287 students, and of these, 85 became Arians or full-blown Unitarians in church ministry.[43] How do we explain this huge rise in heresy? The major factor was the influence of Belsham himself, who was on the same journey to unbelief as his own students during this time. Whereas, as we have seen, Doddridge would freely offer his orthodox opinions, Belsham appeared to extend the degree of free enquiry. David L. Wykes has this to say of Belsham:[44]

> Belsham … updated the theology course … He collected all the passages from the Old and New Testament relating to the person of Christ, to which he added comments from the leading Trinitarian, Arian, and Socinian writers, to provide his students with an impartial view of the subject. To Belsham's dismay, he unintentionally converted most of them to Unitarianism, and in time himself.

It is no surprise to find that the student reading list, which in Doddridge's time had contributions from heterodox authors such as Samuel Clarke, William Whiston and Thomas Emlyn, was further expanded in this direction with unfortunate consequences.

The Unitarian break away movement and its feisty champions

While Presbyterian churches were in decline, there were those who felt an entirely new direction was needed for those who were dissatisfied with Trinitarian belief. Foremost among these was the highly influential Joseph Priestley (1733–1804). Priestley was a brought up in a Calvinistic Dissenter's home. He was a very precocious lad. It is said of him:[45]

> At four years of age Joseph could repeat the Assembly's Catechism without missing a word. When about six and a

half, he would now and then ask a relation to kneel down with him while he prayed.

From precocious infancy Priestley developed into feisty, free-thinking adulthood. From the age of 18 Priestley was educated at the Daventry academy immediately after Doddridge's death. He relished the free enquiry encouraged there, and later became both a distinguished scientist (the discoverer of oxygen, a Fellow of the Royal Society) as well as a controversialist on a huge range of subjects, but especially on those relating to Rational Dissent. His view was that Christ's authority was not mediated through the church but via the individual's reason and conscience. He proposed a complete break from current church structures and ministry, with small groups of laymen worshipping, using a liturgy and printed sermons. He teamed up with Theophilus Lindsey (1723–1808) who had seceded from the Church of England and supported him in opening the first avowedly non-Trinitarian church in England, at Essex Street in London. Priestley was a vigorous campaigner by nature and encouraged his followers to press the government on all matters relating to civil or religious liberty, whether by the printed or spoken word.

It was Priestley with Lindsey who proposed the term Unitarian to describe their system of belief. This was a clever ploy, designed to achieve two things: firstly, to deliver his followers from the correct, but derogatory term Socinian; and secondly, to provide a term which sounded authentic and non-threatening, just a variation on Trinitarian.

In his later battles with Priestley's avowed followers, Herrick refused to use this term, claiming it was nonsense. Here are his forthright words:[46]

This denomination is, like all their proceedings, deceitful.

For I would ask, in what respect are they 'Unitarians,' who deny the unity of three persons in the One Jehovah? The term unity must imply a union of two or more persons or things: and how this can be assumed as the distinctive title of a body of men who maintain that there is but one person in the Godhead, I cannot explain. To talk of the unity of one appears to me very absurd. I think that, so far as the name implies the unity of the Divine Essence, we are more justly entitled to the distinction it imports; nor can I persuade myself to call a Socinian a Unitarian; for the name is improper; and I like to call things by their proper names.

Herrick is right, of course, but we will generally keep to the term Unitarian, as the term Socinian has fallen into disuse.

The Unitarian movement needed a theologian, and they found just the right person in Thomas Belsham (1750–1829). The path of this poor man from orthodox Dissent to heterodox Unitarianism is a sad one indeed. His conscience was violated again and again, but peace was achieved at the end, at the expense of a conscience seared with a hot iron. It was Belsham who re-translated the New Testament in 1808, adding copious notes with a Unitarian bias. To maintain their opinions, which were always claimed to be scriptural, the scriptures themselves had to be changed. We find, long before the Jehovah's Witnesses produced their Bible, Belsham mangling the words of scripture or changing the obvious meaning in his notes.

People with non-Trinitarian beliefs were emboldened by such able champions, and now they had a Bible of their own which explained away orthodox beliefs regarding the person and work of Christ. Just one thing more was needed to put them on a level playing field with orthodox Dissenters: the law against them needed to be changed.

Unitarian Relief and Unitarian Publishing

From around 1790 till 1810 there was a united effort made by Unitarians to give themselves more religious freedom. Two further champions in their ranks were a great help in this. William Smith (1756–1835) had been influenced in favour of Unitarianism through his training at the liberal Daventry Academy in the 1770s. He became a member of Essex Street Unitarian church and a Whig MP in 1784. Non-Trinitarian worship, though at this stage widely accepted, was officially against the law. Smith was a social reformer and he pushed the government for toleration of Unitarian worship to be enshrined by law. Unsuccessful in the 1790s, he was greatly helped by Robert Aspland (1782–1845) in the 1810s. Aspland became a very successful publisher of Unitarian doctrine, with the magazine, *The Monthly Repository* in 1806. His pamphlets in favour of more religious liberty helped Smith in eventually getting the Doctrine of the Trinity Act 1813, known as 'Mr William Smith's Bill', passed. This, for the first time, made it legal to practice Unitarianism. Shortly after the act became law, Aspland started another influential publication: the *Christian Reformer, or New Evangelical Miscellany*. The titles of both his publications give no hint as to their true content: a feature of Unitarian writing at the time Herrick first came on the scene.

Conclusions about the strength of Unitarianism when Herrick entered Colchester

In conclusion, we can see that the Unitarian cause was flexing its muscles around 1814, with the law on its side, voluble champions displaying its merits, excellent publicity and even its own version of the New Testament to argue from.

God-sent revival brings about a collision with error

By the middle of the 18th century, true believers were wondering whether the nation had gone so far in sin and degradation, that all hope of spiritual reformation was lost. Skeats comments in his history:[47]

> To the mass of the people, indeed, religion was almost unknown. Their morals were, for the most part, more degraded than those of beasts. Drunkenness was not merely not frowned upon: it was fashionable. 'I remember,' said Dr Johnson, 'when all the decent people in Lichfield got drunk every night and were not thought the worse for it. The people of Wales and Cornwall were little better than heathens ...

The scriptural answer to this terrible situation is the second phrase of Isaiah 59:19: 'When the enemy comes in like a flood, The Spirit of the LORD will lift up a standard against him.' When everything seemed bleak, God raised up men throughout the British Isles, independently of each other to begin with; men who fearlessly raised the banner of the gospel. Their names are famous now: people such as George Whitefield, John Cennick and John and Charles Wesley in England; Howell Harris and Daniel Rowland in Wales, and many, many others, not forgetting grand supporters like Selena the Countess of Huntingdon.

The response of the Dissenting churches to revival under Whitefield and Wesley differed widely. The heterodox Presbyterian ministers and congregations, with their rational views and cold intellectual approach to religion, were suspicious. Along with liberal Anglicans, they dismissed the 'Methodists,' as they were called, as 'enthusiasts.' Their churches continued their downward path, losing vast numbers of hearers, many of them to liberal Anglican churches where the preacher would lull them to sleep with social homilies which never challenged the conscience. The New Testament describes such people: they were like the Greeks to whom the preaching of the cross was foolishness. Gospel preachers were 'an aroma of death unto death,' to them, as described in 2 Corinthians 2:15,16. The gospel condemned them in their unbelief and rebellion against the truth.

What a contrast with the reaction of most of the Independent and sound Baptist churches! Bogue and Bennett tell us:[48]

> Mr Whitefield was a man of most extensive and beneficial influence; for his mode of preaching has been in some degree adopted by most of the Calvinists in England, to whatever denomination they belonged, but especially by the evangelical clergy and the Independents. The dry, stiff method (of preaching) which too much prevailed under the former period, gave place to that plain, serious, affectionate, and zealous manner which had so eminently distinguished a Baxter, a Flavel and their fellow labourers; and of which Mr Whitefield furnished so splendid an example. From hence originated that homely, straightforward, and pointed address to the consciences of men, and those continued exhortations to impenitent sinners to 'seek the salvation of their souls,' which were so powerful in their effects, both in attracting hearers to the Dissenting places of worship, and in fixing them there, by fixing the principles of the Gospel in their hearts.

It was this amazing work of grace that revived both the evangelical wing of the Church of England as well as the Independent churches and was responsible for the planting of so many new Congregational places of worship. There was a renewed urgency in evangelism: village open air preaching was much increased; saved men were asking to go into pastoral ministry and new evangelical academies were springing up to meet the demand. From these excellent training colleges, hundreds of preachers launched forth with the gospel into cities, towns and villages throughout the land. In many places they came into contact with liberal preachers trained at academies like Daventry, Hackney, Taunton, Exeter, Warrington and Manchester. A battle for truth was inevitable.

The collision between truth and error is not often in the open. In Colchester, as in other towns and villages, Unitarians often hid their true beliefs under a veneer of social respectability. They may have been encouraged by Priestley and his followers to be more open, but boldness was not always in their blood. The next chapters describe how this battle played out in Colchester.

Chapter 4
Colchester's Dissenting churches before Herrick's arrival

As for so many ministers in England, 24 May, 1662 was an ominous day for the men responsible for Colchester's two main churches. Edward Warren was the minister of St Peters at the top of North Hill; Owen Stockton the vicar of St James at the top of East Hill. Their church buildings were only the length of the High Street apart—a mere quarter of a mile. They knew each other well; they were gospel men. Calamy, a Presbyterian minister of the time, said of Stockton's arrival in Colchester in the late 1650s:[49]

> His very first sermon was blessed to the conversion of one who heard it, and his second or third to that of another who was noted as a very profligate sinner, and who came from mere curiosity to hear him.

Of Warren he said:[50]

> He was a pious and learned divine, a man of singular abilities, good elocution and great humility.

Now they were united in adversity. On that very day they were both thrown out of their vicarages and church buildings for refusing to use the new prayer book and all the detritus of Popish ceremony which went with it. They were now cast on the Lord, determined in His strength to work together to maintain a gospel witness in the town.

Both men were Cambridge graduates: Warren a Presbyterian at heart, Stockton an Independent. The two ministers and their people worshipped together where and when they could. Stockton used his own house for this purpose for three years until the town constable put an end to it, just at the point when the town was afflicted with the plague. Things improved in 1672 when permission was granted to licence buildings for the purpose of worship. Stockton, from this point, served a congregation in Ipswich as well as in Colchester. Warren, earned his living as a physician, while sharing the preaching duties with Stockton. This happy state of affairs continued with Independents and Presbyterians meeting together in a room in Colchester Castle. Stockton died in 1680, but Warren continued to share duties with Stockton's successor William Folkes until his own death in 1690.

Separate Independent and Presbyterian churches

When more religious liberty was given under king William in 1689, Independent and Presbyterian congregations could meet separately in their own meeting rooms. The Independents had separated from the Established church as early as 1640 and after the death of Warren they divided into two congregations under pastors of the Independent (Congregational) church order. By the time Herrick arrived there was one well-attended Congregational church in Colchester, meeting in Lion's Walk.

In 1691 the Presbyterians built a large Meeting Room in Bucklersbury Lane (currently St Helens Lane—from now on, Helens Lane for short). This had the capacity for a congregation of around 600 people, and under their first minister Daniel Gilson (1657–1728) there were as many as 1,500 hearers,[51] (totalled over the three meetings on the Lord's Day.) Of this faithful man of God, we are told:[52]

> An earnest and sincere desire of promoting the divine glory, and furthering the salvation of souls, breathed forth in all his sermons ... So much was his heart set upon his

Master's work that he went through the greatest difficulties
… He preached when in danger of imprisonment …
ascended the pulpit when his friends thought him, through
bodily weakness unable to bear up.

Free thinking in religion begins

At his death in 1728 Gilson had ministered for 37 years. He was
succeeded by his assistant of many years, John Tren. This man
served for 10 years and left written sermons which indicate the
issues of the day and the way they were treated. One
particularly interesting one was preached on November 5,
1732. It was a heartfelt plea against any sort of persecution,
bringing to vivid remembrance the Gunpowder plot and the
fiery martyrdoms of Mary's reign. It gave effusive thanks for
the freedoms enjoyed under William of Orange and pleaded for
further freedom by the repeal of the Test and Corporation Acts
which so limited the Dissenters in education and employment.
Of particular interest was a plea for freedom of conscience in
doctrinal matters:[53]

> … it is next to one, if it be not an absolute impossibility, for
> all men to be of the same mind and judgment in all religious
> matters. God nowhere commands us to be so, only with
> respect to the main principles of religion.

> One way of expressing a spirit of persecution is by words
> … The spirit of persecution in this manner prevails and is too
> visible among all parties. Why else do we hear the terms,
> Deist, Socinian, Arian, Arminian, Calvinist, Antinomian, and
> such like, so often bandied about in conversation, and
> applied to particular persons? What end can men have in so
> doing, but to point out such and such persons to the world
> as dangerous, and infectious; who ought to be avoided as

carefully as those who have got the plague.

Surely a true gospel man *would* avoid contact with doctrinal errors like Arianism and Socinianism which so denigrate the person and work of Jesus Christ. Tren's comments suggest some freedom in doctrinal thinking in Helens Lane at this time. This reflects the way Presbyterian congregations were going after the Salters Hall watershed discussed in Chapter 3.

The first unorthodox men minister at Helens Lane

Bearing this in mind, it is perhaps not a shock to find that the next three holders of the pastoral office were Arian if not full-blown Unitarians in their doctrinal position. The three men were: Richard Harrison, Charles Bulkley, and James Gillibrand. Their pastorates were mercifully very short, covering between them the years 1738 to 1741. Richard Harrison had been trained at the notorious Taunton Academy and he is described as having definite Unitarian sympathies as well as not being a popular preacher.[54] Nothing is known of Gillibrand, but Charles Bulkley's is a sad case. He was a grandson of the saintly Matthew Henry and had trained for the ministry under Philip Doddridge at his academy in Northampton. Here were Doddridge's thoughts on this unfortunate man, expressed in a letter to Isaac Watts:[55]

Mr. C. B.'s Distortion of mind ... first arose from ungoverned love ... Love produced indolence, neglect of study, and ... chat, disputation, indevotion, pride, and error. I write this with grief of heart ... I have always had a peculiar tenderness for this unhappy lad, and yet, after all, see him in a great measure spoiled and ruined under my most affectionate care. Yet I am not altogether without hopes as to his recovery ... I have stated what appears to me the truth with the utmost evidence I could give ... I have ... most affectionately, and often with many tears, represented the importance of adhering to the simplicity of the gospel with steadiness and zeal, and of maintaining that holy and watchful course of walking with God ... To all this I have added, as soon as I heard of his defection, personal admonition, earnest prayer to God for him ... I have recommended him to God even with paternal affection. If, after all this, he turns out, with all his excellent and popular talents, an Arian, a Socinian, or a Pelagian, I hope I may say, I have delivered my own soul.

Sadly, there is no evidence that Bulkley recovered from his errors.

After this three-year hiatus, an orthodox minister by the name of James Throgmorton settled from 1742 to 1753, and the church appears to have flourished, with the need for six deacons to assist the minister.

The long doctrinal decline begins

Throgmorton's death in 1753 marked the beginning of a long period of decline for Helens Lane, covering the next 42 years. Some difficulty was experienced in obtaining a minister. The Lion Walk congregation (at that point still meeting in Moor Lane) at one point in 1754 invited a young man called Wren to preach to them. The minister, Ebenezer Cornell, was quite scathing, both of his unengaging style of preaching, and the Arian tendency of his theology.[56] Helens Lane, however, were happy to use his services for a short time. A little while later they chose the first of a succession of three ministers with strong Unitarian sympathies: Thomas Stanton, William Waters and Rees Harris. Herrick said of Stanton that:[57]

He declared enmity to the doctrines of the Cross, kindled the flames of controversy, gave the people a relish for error and planted the deadly upas (poisonous Ed.) tree of Socinianism ...

It is difficult to understand how a church which had enjoyed gospel preaching could choose such unsatisfactory ministers. The root of the problem probably lay with the method Presbyterian churches used in searching for and approving new pastors. The selection process seems to have rested on the shoulders of trustees and subscribers, rather than church members. Some, if not many of these, could be unregenerate men who owed their position to wealth and position in society. What criteria they used in inviting ministers, even at the point when Herrick came, we do not know: doctrinal belief appeared to be low on the list.

The table below summarises the list of ministers in Helens Lane up to the point when Rees Harris resigned the pastorate in 1795.

Name	Dates	Association
Edward Warren	1672 – 1690	Presbyterian
Daniel Gilson	1691 – 1728	Presbyterian
John Tren	1728 – 1738	Presbyterian
Richard Harrison	c. 1738	Unitarian
Charles Bulkley	c. 1739	Unitarian
James Gillibrand	c. 1741	Unitarian
James Throgmorton	1742 – 1753	Presbyterian
? Wren	c. 1754	Unitarian
Thomas Stanton	1754 – 1776	Unitarian
William Waters	1776 – 1782	Unitarian
Rees Harris	1783 - 1795	Unitarian

Table 2: Ministers of Helens Lane 1672 to 1795

Herrick is biting in his criticism of the last of these men, Rees Harris:[58]

He was a man of no religion, and therefore fell a prey to the temptation of sociality, and at his farewell adopted the following text as the ground for his discourse: 'I was a reproach among all mine enemies, but especially among my neighbours, and a fear to mine acquaintance: they that did see me fled from me.' Psalm 31:11.

It appears that Harris resigned his office when he found that everyone in the church was anxious for him to go.[59]

An orthodox pastor tries unavailingly to turn around Helens Lane

In November 1795, what promised to be a brighter time for Helens Lane began. The church invited a deacon from a Congregational church in Lavenham, in Suffolk, to supply for them: Isaac Taylor. The officers of the church were sufficiently encouraged by December to ask him to act as their pastor. Accordingly, church and pastor were joined together at an ordination ceremony on April 21, 1796.

The extract below shows the start of the old church minute book at the point of Isaac Taylor's arrival.

Taylor was aware of the low condition of the church, as is evident from the comments of his daughter Ann:[60]

> There was at the time … a small congregation of Presbyterian origin, which had degenerated into a condition, not so intellectual, but as cold as Unitarianism. There was a good building, some small endowment, and two or three substantial families; while a return to something like evangelical sentiments seemed the only chance of revival.

For the first four years until 1800 the cause did seem to revive. Twenty-eight new members were received into church fellowship,[61] a happy spirit seemed to pervade the company of believers, new members spoke of the blessing they received under the preached word of God:[62]

> Mrs Margaret Rouse … had for nearly two years past found the preaching of the word among us … so much blessed to her soul's spiritual nourishment that she could no longer rest easy nor be satisfied in conscience without an entire attendance with us.

Sadly, the cause changed dramatically in the last ten years of Taylor's ministry. In the years from 1801 to 1810 only three new members were added; many older members died, and the regular monthly meetings for church business were held every quarter till the end of 1805, and then only yearly after that. Margaret Rouse, so keen for membership in 1799, asked for her name to be erased in May 1808; this after she had tried her pastor's patience to the limit with her disorderly behaviour.[63]

Other factors contributed to the decline in Helens Lane in the early 1800s. Because of the paucity of conversions, the attention of members was drawn away to practical matters. First, the trusteeship of the chapel had declined to only two people. To remedy this, 15 new church trustees were chosen from a pool of 25 men: some members, others just subscribers. Some of these were those who caused trouble soon after Herrick arrived. Secondly, it transpired that the building itself had been neglected: there was no fire insurance; painting or decorating had been neglected for 40 years, and serious cracks were beginning to appear in the walls. In addition to this repair work, it was decided to re-arrange the pews—something that upsets congregations even today. During the upheaval this necessary work entailed and the extra financial burden on everyone, members began to leave. Eleven members out of a small membership numbering in the forties departed, some to the local parish church, others to the Baptists, others sadly for good. The minute book chronicles a church in serious decline.

A clue as to the state of heart of Colchester's Dissenters comes from the writings of Isaac Taylor's daughter Ann (Ann Gilbert when she later married). This is her comment on church life in Colchester when the family came to town:[64]

> The number of chapels, at the time we knew Colchester, was small. Dissent there was not many-headed, but neither was it intelligent, nor of a sort to promise increase. There was a tendency to 'high doctrine,' (leaving a low sediment,) in most of the congregations. In the large old 'Round Meeting,' [i.e. Lion Walk Congregational Church, Ed.] holding about a thousand people, and generally well filled, there was an elderly, heavy, unattractive minister[65] under the singular chant of whose slow, monotonous delivery the young people of his charge just thought their own thoughts and considered they had paid sufficient respect to Sunday. Indeed, so sad was the state of things when we entered Colchester, that no young person of good education, position, and intelligence, was associated in the

membership of any Nonconformist church in the town. In our own congregation there were a few substantial families, and two or three wealthy individuals, but these were the only present materials. The dissenters of the town were men of habit more than men of piety, and few knew or thought why they dissented. This condition, however, did not continue; many felt there was a reason before they saw it, and the consciousness of a principle came at last. Among the twelve churches in the town the ministrations at one only were accounted evangelical, at that time the sole form of life in the Establishment, and the abilities of the clergyman officiating there, excellent man as he was, were about as commonplace as were likely to obtain holy orders. Of the clergyman of our own parish, the Rev. Yorick Smythies, I can only record the sacerdotal-looking but very portly figure, the rotundity of which was the more striking, from his habit of walking with his hands behind him, and which occasioned at last his melancholy end; for not observing thereby an open cellar, he fell into it, and was killed! 'Alas, poor Yorick!'

Ann Gilbert was a godly woman, who knew and loved the gospel. This is evident from her glorious Trinitarian hymn, 'What was it, O our God, led Thee to give Thy Son,' still sung today.

Ann Gilbert also knew from personal experience the deadly effects of Unitarianism. She and her sister Jane had made friends with three girls in a local family, the Stapletons. Letitia the eldest was closest to Jane, Bithia the youngest to Ann, while Mira was a friend to both. In the early 1800s the three girls had been sent to Dublin where they were introduced to sophisticated relatives who encouraged them in the soul-sapping doctrines of Unitarianism. This made them feel rather superior, and friendly relations with the Taylor girls were discouraged. In a few short years all three Stapleton girls were dying from consumption. The contrast in their death bed statements is highly instructive. Ann comments on the death of Bithia:[66]

> In one of her last (letters) to me she said, 'do you think I can be saved by Christ without believing on him?' Sad to lie down and die on such a precipice!

Mira's last words were perhaps equally sad:[67]

> A single sentence only reached us from her dying words, indicating conflicting thoughts, 'Lord save me in thine own way!'

How different it was with Letitia. Conscious of having turned from her only Saviour God, she was in an agony of fear in case she died without hope. God was gracious and granted a full repentance. She completely renounced all trust in the illusions that had deceived her, and now were quite unable to satisfy her awakened conscience. Jane says of her:[68]

> ... the whole temper of her mind was renovated; she became patient, thankful, affectionate, and humble; and triumphed in the profession of her hope. 'My hope,' she said, 'is in Christ—in Christ crucified—and I would not give up that hope, for all the world!

It was the Unitarian doctrine, bereft of both a Divine Saviour and his atonement, which was freezing the life out of Helens Lane, as it had done in countless churches throughout England.

Members at Helens Lane were probably no more than closet Unitarians at this time: unwilling to openly admit their allegiance, but creating an atmosphere of deadness, and a darkness that could be felt. Ann Gilbert indicates another serious issue in the churches too. Years without the gospel had led some to high, Hypercalvinistic views. It was this that led Isaac Taylor in 1810 to conclude his work at Colchester was finished. The effect these views had on some of his flock is indicated in this quote from Ann Gilbert:[69]

> A letter from Mr Taylor to a friend illustrates the nature of the evil he had to contend with, a leaven of Antinomianism which seems to have troubled several of the small Essex churches at that time, and which could not brook his earnest exhortations to personal holiness, nor the strict church discipline he enforced … One of them, when speaking of low frames and worldliness of mind, instead of being humbled and ashamed, took his comfort thus: 'If God don't choose to give me grace for better living, how can I help it?' They commonly held that a believer ought not to pray for the pardon of sins, because they are already pardoned; and when reminded of the practice of the apostles, had the insolence to reply that if the apostles did not understand their own doctrines better, that was no rule for us! Now, as they held also, that it was of no use for a sinner to pray at all, because unable to any spiritual exertion, they shut out prayer for pardon entirely.

Helens Lane descends even lower

It is difficult to see how the situation at Helens Lane could have got any worse, yet within 18 months it did. Isaac Taylor informed the church of his determination to resign in midsummer 1810 but gave the officers plenty of notice by continuing to preach for them till the end of September. The church acted swiftly, obtaining Joseph Drake on probation for three months before offering him the pastorate on December 23, 1810. Joseph Drake was a Congregational minister characterised as a good preacher, fearless in declaring the truth.[70] He was inducted into the role on March 27, 1811. We are told of him that he had:[71]

Some peculiarities of temper (which) occasioned him frequent disquietude in his pastoral relations.

In the case of Helens Lane, he had every right to be 'disquieted' by the events of 1811. Things seemed to start well, with 9 new members joining the church within the first 5 months. Then disaster struck. In August 1811, ten members, a mix of Antinomians and closet Unitarians, had the temerity to force into the pulpit a preacher of their own choosing, with the utter disapproval of the pastor and other members. This man was John Church, a practising homosexual from a London church, Obelisk Chapel, St Georges Field. Whether the men who invited him were totally aware of his proclivities it is difficult to establish. Rumours of his behaviour in a Banbury church had been circulating since 1808, and Herrick in the church minute book of 1814, calls him 'an Antinomian preacher of very vile character.' In 1821 Herrick denotes him:[72] 'a wretch in form human, but in his nature so vile that it would dishonour the most unclean beast to compare him to it.' Joseph Drake left the church on 23, December 1811, after what Herrick calls 'cruel usage.'

This intrusion of John Church was referred to in a letter which J.B. Harvey (one of the later Colchester greats) pasted into one of his scrapbooks. The letter was written on August 16, 1811 and the writer pokes fun at the whole incident:[73]

This week has been remarkable for the appearance of a blazing meteor, I do not say star, which has attracted the attention of most ranks of people in this neighbourhood. It has chiefly hovered over Barren Heath, Man's Field, Pat Moor, and a few more uncultivated spots, and in the opinion of some persons, is not a little indebted to the stagnant water of an adjacent waste ground for its brilliancy. Like an Ignus Fatus[74] it has led some of them they know not where; and so disordered are their intellects that they are determined to call mystic wilderness by the name of wisdom's way—This phenomenon is beginning to wane but whether at its disappearance the people will return to their duty and allegiance to their rightful guide, time only will discover, at present they are the people, and wisdom is to die with them.

The three capitalised names refer to three well known Dissenters connected to Helens Lane: Mansfield, Patmore and Heath. (J.B. Harvey wrongly tells us that this incident refers to Herrick himself. This would have been quite impossible in a month when John Church was preaching and before Herrick was even in the county. John Hubbard's signature is written in pencil at the base of the excerpt, suggesting he was either the writer or the recipient of the letter).

Unconcerned by the loss of Drake, the deviant members caused further chaos in Helens Lane: John Church was invited again in February 1812! The meeting room had to be locked against him, while the more orthodox members called on the local mayor for his henchmen to protect them. Peace was eventually restored when the ten decided to withdraw from Helens Lane and seek a place of their own. The utter hypocrisy of their letter of withdrawal can be seen below:[75]

Dear friends   Colchester 28th Feb, 1812

... (as) we profess to be followers of the meek and lowly Jesus, we conceive we should not act like Christians if we were to make use of carnal weapons to retain our place of worship, and as two cannot walk together unless they be agreed, we think it our duty to say farewell; wishing you a minister after God's own heart, who may break to you the

Bread of Life. It's not for us to say who have been the aggressors, God will decide that question another day, we will retire and pray for you and hope you will pray for us and may you do all in your power to weaken Satan's kingdom and we will in the strength of Grace make the attack, in the humble spot which providence may provide for us.

Charles Heath—Deacon	John Nickels
John Hubbard—Deacon	The mark of x Mary Emery
Thomas Inman	Mary Clarke
John Danford	Elizabeth Inman
Charles Abbot	Hannah Danford

One would hope this was the last we heard of these people— but not so. Astonishingly, the first three names in the left-hand column reappear as trustees of the chapel in 1815!

Conclusion on the state of Helens Lane when Herrick arrived

It is difficult to imagine a more trying set of circumstances for a young pastor to cope with on joining a church. One could believe this to be quite the worst church in the land. One good man had tried for 15 years to turn it round and resigned in frustration and disappointment. The next pastor, another excellent preacher, survived for a mere 9 months. Before these two good men, the church had been fed a starvation diet of Unitarianism for over 40 years continuously; many of the more senior members had been there for a large part of this time. What hope could there be of a change? The answer of course is, 'with God all things are possible.' Our Saviour acts in grace, 'he does not reward us according to our iniquities.' Yet God uses means; he uses instruments. God had prepared a very decided character in Joseph Herrick; a man with a strong constitution and much firmness. God especially gave a man whom God would enable to take all the fiery darts of the wicked one, and yet having done all to stand in the strength God alone can supply. What is more, he came with an utter conviction of the saving truths of the gospel, and a burning desire to offer this salvation to all. The deadening effects of both Hypercalvinism and Unitarianism were anathema to him—other gospels totally devoid of good news for the sinner. The churches in London to which Herrick had belonged after his conversion were derived from, if not directly connected to, George Whitefield and the Calvinistic Methodists. Thomas Wilson, to whom he looked so often for advice, had the same theology, both his parents having been saved under Whitefield's preaching at Moorfield's Tabernacle. All his life Herrick was a preacher with Whitefield's convictions: declaiming the gospel to all strata of society. This was the gospel which was so evidently lacking in Colchester in the early 1800s.

Not everyone was sure that Helens Lane was the right church for Herrick. The minister of Lion Walk Independent Church in Colchester, Rev. John Savill, warned Herrick on December 23, 1813:

Visited Mr Savill who treated me very kindly but gave me no hope of a comfortable settlement with the people of Helens Lane.

Even Thomas Wilson was disapproving at the beginning but saw the wisdom of the move before very long.

Chapter 5
Herrick's first year at Helens Lane

Probationary preacher and ordination

The church to which Joseph Herrick came in December 1813 was in disarray. The more orthodox of the remaining church members (only 18 in number) had attempted to persuade Joseph Drake to stay on, but to no avail. During 1812 and 1813 the church had invited students from Hoxton academy to supply the pulpit, but none of them, understandably, wanted the pastor's role.[76] The first Herrick entry in the old church minute book is shown here in his distinctive script:

> *The Church Book – Recommenced.*
> *By Joseph Herrick,*
> *Pastor of ÿ Church of X.t. in Helens Lane Colchester*
> *April – Anno Domini – One thousand eight hundred & 14 –*

> This Church was thrown into a great deal of confusion in the year 1810 By a m.r Church, an Antinomian Preacher, of very vile character, being forced into ÿ Pulpit contrary to the wish of the Generality of the People — The confusion terminated in the loss of their Pastor ÿ Rev.d Joseph Drake, who resigned his charge on ÿ 25 of December 1811 — see memorandum in the Book
> "The Church was then supplied with students from ÿ Academy
> "at Hoxton for about two Years. During this time several
> "meetings were called with ÿ view of inviting one of them
> "to ÿ Pastoral Charge — but every effort proved ineffective
> "al, all their designs seemed frustrated almost as soon
> "as they were formed" — copied from ÿ paper read by James Marshal
> Sen.r On ÿ Day of m.r Herrick's Ordination. —
> In December 1813. M.r Herrick came down from London
> Recommended by M.r Thomas Wilson, Treasurer of ÿ Hoxton
> Academy — & preached his first Sermon on Xmas day,
> Dec 25 — After labouring amongst them for three weeks,
> He received an invitation to preach amongst them 3 Months

Herrick arrived in Colchester on 22 December, 1813. Despite little encouragement from pastor John Savill of the Lion Walk church, he threw himself into the God-given opportunity for service with all the energy he could muster. In the first 16 days, he preached at Helens Lane no less than 10 times. This included three sermons on the second Lord's Day, 2 January, 1814, with two engagements at the Wednesday evening lecture as it was known. In between he had done a full round of visiting church members; gone to Grays to explain his new situation (and nearly been killed in his chaise when his horse fell in deep snow on his return); written a letter to his fiancée Ann Douglas and replied to a trying missive from his mentor Thomas Wilson; attended meetings at both the Baptist and Lion Walk Congregational churches, and fitted in his regular study, reading, and meals. After only three weeks at Helens Lane, Herrick received a request from the chief members and subscribers of the church, asking him to preach on probation for three months. After prayerful consideration, Herrick accepted the call and on 27 April, 1814 he was ordained on 'the most memorable day of his life.'

He wrote in his diary:

I this day gave myself up to God and my people. The service was very solemn, my mind was very much affected. Almighty God, let not the impression ever be erased, but so long as I live, I remember this solemn and interesting epoch of my life, and be enabled as I this day resolved, to devote the residue of my days to him who I believe snatched me as a brand from the burning. O Lord God Almighty, succeed my efforts, make me a good minister of Jesus Christ, let much good be done in his name.

The scriptures exhort us: 'Whatever your hand finds to do, do it with your might.' Ecclesiastes 9:10. Herrick obeyed this command throughout his Christian life. Its application to his situation at Helens Lane began immediately. He preached around 20 times a month, visiting all his people very regularly, 'studying to make himself approved unto God,' as well as devouring Christian books and other general literature which might enliven his sermons. In a typical month he would read 1200 pages, but this climbed to over 2000 pages in a month when he was not travelling. On top of this he chaired the monthly church meeting and kept an accurate record of people joining or leaving and discussions carried out.

Marriage to Ann Douglas

A few years before, while he still lived in London, Herrick had come to know Ann Douglas, the daughter of John Douglas, the goldsmith to whom he was apprenticed. Ann was born on 4 September, 1791 to John and Sarah Douglas, who lived in Clerkenwell. John Douglas came from a godly Dissenting family. John's parents had been encouraged by the fact that his two older brothers had entered Congregational Church ministry: Samuel at Chelmsford and Archibald at Reading. It seems highly likely that John and Sarah Douglas were believers: Ann was baptized as a baby by Stephen Addington while he was pastor of Miles Lane Congregational Church, London, so presumably the family were members there. Joseph and Ann fell in love and entered some sort of engagement during his apprenticeship.

During the busy period at Grays and then Colchester many letters were exchanged, and Ann is referred to consistently as 'my dear Ann.' Being away from home, and away from his sweetheart was a trial to Herrick. The earliest engraving of Herrick at the age of 32 shows quite a handsome young man.

Rev.ᵈ Jas.ᵗ Herrick

Colchester.

Figure 5: Portrait of Herrick from 1826[77]

While he was on his own in Colchester, Herrick visited many families as part of his pastoral work. These were not all families of church members; some were subscribers, some members of other local Dissenting churches. As a bachelor, he was introduced to eligible young ladies. It was during this period that Herrick earned a reputation he would never lose: that of having an almost hypnotic influence over the ladies. There is absolutely no evidence of moral impropriety at any period of his life, but people noticed, and many years later some of the men felt the influence of the women was too great in church meetings and took measures to curb it.

Herrick confesses his failings in this respect in his diary:

Miss Rouse struck my fancy so much that I felt it move me to acts of kindness which I ought not to think of because I am as solemnly engaged to my dear Ann as though I was already married.

Miss Rouse was not the only alternative lady to whom he felt attracted at this stage. Two months later he confessed that he felt uneasy in the presence of Maria Walford, even to the point of wondering whether he was that concerned about maintaining his attachment to his betrothed.

The competition for his heart was decided by an exchange of letters; one in the middle of this period is referred to in touching terms in his diary:

Received ... from London, a letter from my very dear Ann, it brought tears to my eyes. She reminded me of my sorrow about two years ago for fear I should lose her. Blessed be God for sparing a life so dear to me, Lord. Cut us not off in the midst of our days! Make us happy with each other in time and happy with thee in eternity.

In May of 1814, Herrick went to London to see Ann and ask her father for her hand in marriage. He had a struggle at first to convince John Douglas: one imagines the financial prospects of a minister could hardly match that of a jeweller, but agree he did in the end.

The wedding took place on 1 June, 1814. In his typically matter of fact way, Herrick records the event in his diary:

> June 1, 1814. This day an important change has taken place in my life. I was married by licence to Miss Ann Douglas at St. John's church, Clerkenwell. Drove from London to Colchester, home about 9. Almighty God! Grant that our union may be productive of much lasting happiness to us both, for thy mercy's sake, Amen.

There was no luxury allowed for a honeymoon: straight back to work, preaching twice in the chapel the next Lord's Day; but there is an admission that he was 'very much fatigued' by the end of all this.

Ann was a very loyal wife to Joseph, but she never enjoyed good health. He relates in his poetic sketches:[78]

> But though I much domestic peace enjoy,
> I have my troubles, oft I'm racked with fear,
> Lest I should lose my love, my life, my joy;
> The only object which to me is dear.

> My wife, the subject of capricious health,
> Is oft oppressed with languor and disease.
> I ofttimes think had I a monarch's wealth,
> I'd part with all that she might live in ease.

Establishing church order: a proper diaconate

The New Testament shows the ideal pattern of local church order with elders and deacons among a body of believing people. Most Congregational churches of the time were close to the Biblical model. They had a paid minister as the teaching elder and pastor. They also had one or more deacons who really functioned as elders in that their chief work was spiritual. They were involved in visiting and interviewing potential new church members, as well as assisting the pastor in his care of the flock.

Helens Lane had the remnants of this structure; it was one of Herrick's first tasks to encourage the church to move more in line with scripture. Before his first church meeting, Herrick suspected there was a problem with the diaconate. The issue concerned the behaviour of the sole surviving deacon, Mr James Mansfield senior, a man already around 80 years of age when Herrick came.

Mansfield senior was a wealthy man of some property, involved in the manufacture of coarse baize cloth from wool. A widower since 1804,[79] he had a large, well-connected family: his two sons James junior and Samuel, intimately connected with the church as well as his married daughter Mary Wright. Like many families long associated with one church, there were cousins, aunts and uncles as well. Isaac Taylor never had serious misgivings about Mansfield during his pastorate, and Ann Gilbert his daughter calls him 'a worthy man.'[80] He evidently used his money in subscriptions to the church, and while Herrick was still a bachelor invited him most weeks for meals with his family. However, within the first month at Colchester, Herrick felt something was wrong. He confided in his diary:

> Just as I was thinking of going to Mr Mansfield's I received a message by Nevill that I was not to go. What a strange old man. Went to him with Mr J. Thorn. Went to Mrs Tillet. They treat me very shabbily indeed in not providing me with a

lodging ... Very comfortable when I left the pulpit, but on leaving it was given to understand that I was expected to go to Mrs Thorn's whereas Mr Mansfield had faithfully promised again and again that I should go to his house this evening. I am astonished: he has no more regard for his word than for a pin.

Early problems like this made Herrick resolve to do something about the diaconate. He was disturbed by the changeable character of his only deacon, feeling that Mansfield would only cause trouble in the future if he acted alone. He determined to press ahead with forming a group of deacons.

At the very first church meeting in April 1814, Herrick proposed a new deacon, James Nash, to work alongside James Mansfield. From this point on, Mansfield was only asked to visit one prospective new church member—Mrs Ann Herrick in July 1814, whereas Nash and other brethren were used repeatedly. This was undoubtedly intended to limit Mansfield's influence, and must have rankled, but it was effective in bringing out the true character of the man. In March 1815, he refused to sign a dismission of his previous pastor Joseph Drake to another church. From this point on he acted as leader of the opposition to Herrick, as we shall see in the next chapter.

Christian friends and some who opposed

It is very easy for church pastors to become isolated in their church position. Herrick was aware of this problem, especially as he was still only just 20 years old when he was ordained to the pastorate. Sensibly, Herrick established a solid group of Christian friends to whom he could turn for help and advice. This was no easy task. How could he trust church members who had sat under a Unitarian ministry for a significant length of time: the basis of his problem with James Mansfield? The only two Helens Lane families he could depend on were those who became members under the very short pastorate of Joseph Drake and had not had the chance to be damaged by heretical teaching. His closest friends from this group, admitted to fellowship in 1811, were:

> James and Martha Nash,
> Thomas and Dinah Foakes.

James Nash was 25 years older than Herrick, and became his loyal deacon, his chief advisor and warm-hearted friend, a kind of father-figure to whom he could go, especially during the difficult early years. The Foakes's also strongly supported Herrick during those difficult years, but they left Colchester in 1817 and had less of an impact.

There was also a group of Dissenting families who attended the Lion Walk Independent Church in the town and though familiar with the goings on at Helens Lane were not infected with Unitarian or Hypercalvinist errors. The largest of these families was the Rouses. At least three generations of this family lived in Colchester and they all opened their homes to Joseph and Ann and were faithful friends to the end, as far as we can trace. Two other families need to be mentioned. The Walfords were the very first to welcome Herrick on his arrival. Herrick called Mr Walford 'my dear friend,' and the diary still records his name as late as 1858. The Thorns were another large and well-connected family of Independents who did all they could to support Herrick.

In contrast with this group of true friends, we should mention two further couples who proved to be less reliable. Benjamin Baldrey was a subscriber at the time when Herrick was invited to preach on probation, and he and his wife Phanuel became members in August 1814. They were very friendly to begin with, but they came under the influence of James Mansfield and after 12 months they fell out with Herrick and took Mansfield's side in opposing gospel ministry.

George and Ann Lester were friendly to Herrick for a much longer period. They too had been subscribers to Helens Lane when Herrick first came and became full members in August/September of 1814. The Lester 'friendship' seems to have been rather fraught at times. The couples saw far too much of each other: about seven times a month outside the church. The scriptural advice from Proverbs 25:17 is relevant here: 'seldom set foot in your neighbour's house, lest he become weary of you and hate you.' Lester called on Herrick nearly every Saturday evening: not the best time for a man contemplating preaching on the Lord's day. The irritation slips out in the diary just once: 'Lester called *as usual.*' Herrick never called Lester his friend, though he did recognise the couple's acts of kindness, especially when the children were born. Lester seems to have been an earthy, forthright and rather volatile character, in some respects too similar to Herrick. Although the Lesters stood solidly behind Herrick in the Unitarian crisis of 1815–16, there was a serious falling out in the 1820s. Further deacons were employed in this period and Lester found it difficult to work with a more gifted younger man in this capacity. He fell completely out of control and had to be disciplined by the church. Fellowship was later restored, but sadly there was a final separation and much bitterness when the crisis of 1839–43 hit the church.

The start of solid Bible preaching

Although we have no written sermons from Herrick we have a very thorough picture of the scriptural passages he preached from and his comments on the attendance and sometimes the impact that was created. Herrick was primarily a short text preacher—a pattern common in the great Baptist preacher Spurgeon too and popular with many reformed preachers of today.

A major principle in Herrick's preaching was 'deal with doctrinal and behavioural issues as soon as they arise.' While he was still on probation he notes in his diary on March 2, 1814:

Some persons have branded me with the name of Socinian. Lord keep me from all such errors, preserve me from wicked misrepresentations, and support me under all such trials.

Herrick could have just argued against the charge and left it there. Rather, within a week he had bought a 600-page book on the Divinity of Christ—David Simpson's *Plea for the Deity of Jesus*. He read it through, as well the author's subsequent 'Socinianism exemplified.' Having thoroughly prepared his ground he then dealt with the issue head on:

Sunday April 17. (1814) Preached 3 times at Helens Lane, very good congregation in the afternoon, in the evening completely overflowed. I preached on (Matthew 22:42) 'what think ye of Christ?' and hope it will decide the question, to be a Socinian or not. How they could suppose such a thing I know not, unless they think I must be like my predecessors.

Thus, Herrick's preaching dealt with the major doctrinal issue at Helens Lane, ten days before his ordination: quite extraordinary courage!

Another feature of Herrick's preaching was the full-orbed gospel he presented to sinners.

He demonstrated the necessity of hearing and believing God's word from Romans 10:17: 'So then faith comes by hearing, and hearing by the word of God.'

He insisted on the wrath of God against sin, but the wonderful mercy of God in Christ: preaching from Isaiah 54:8: 'With a little wrath I hid My face from you for a moment; But with everlasting kindness I will have mercy on you," says the LORD, your Redeemer,' and from Micah 7:18: 'Who is a God like You, pardoning iniquity and passing over the transgression of the remnant of His heritage? He does not retain His anger forever, because He delights in mercy.'

He proved the necessity of repentance, from texts such as Luke 15:18: 'I will arise and go to my father, and will say to him, "Father, I have sinned against heaven and before you."'

He showed the necessity of faith in Christ's atoning work at Calvary, from a variety of texts including: Luke 23:42: 'Then he said to Jesus, "Lord, remember me when You come into Your kingdom."' Acts 16:31: 'So they said, "Believe on the Lord Jesus Christ, and you will be saved, you and your household,"' and Zechariah 13:1: 'In that day a fountain shall be opened for the house of David and for the inhabitants of Jerusalem, for sin and for uncleanness.'

He urged the need of a new heart from Ezekiel 36:26: 'I will give you a new heart and put a new spirit within you; I will take the heart of stone out of your flesh and give you a heart of flesh.'

He argued against the folly of neglect from Hebrews 2:3: 'how shall we escape if we neglect so great a salvation, which at the first began to be spoken by the Lord and was confirmed to us by those who heard Him.' He records in his diary, after preaching this sermon:

Sunday September 25. Felt very earnestly desirous both today and yesterday, that God would bless my sermon on, 'how shall we escape etc' to the conversion of some poor sinner. O that it might be so!

He comforted the downcast by showing that God will finish the work he begins, preaching from Philippians 1:6: 'being confident of this very thing, that He who has begun a good work in you will complete it until the day of Jesus Christ.'

In all this preaching, believers were not neglected. Not only were they thrilled to hear the gospel, they were guided and encouraged to go on the know the Lord as they were taken through a vast range of Old and New Testament scriptures.

God's sovereign electing love was taught from Romans 9:21: 'Does not the potter have power over the clay, from the same lump to make one vessel for honour and another for dishonour?' And from Revelation 13:8: 'All who dwell on the earth will worship him, whose names have not been written in the Book of Life of the Lamb slain from the foundation of the world.'

God's gracious love to backsliders was preached from Jeremiah 3:12 'Go and proclaim these words toward the north, and say: 'return, backsliding Israel,' says the LORD; 'I will not cause My anger to fall on you. For I am merciful,' says the LORD; 'I will not remain angry forever.'

The comfort of Christ's second coming was applied from 1 Thessalonians 4:17–18 'Then we who are alive and remain shall be caught up together with them in the clouds to meet the Lord in the air. And thus we shall always be with the Lord. Therefore comfort one another with these words.'

The necessity of guarding against bitterness was shown from

Hebrews 12:15 'looking carefully lest anyone fall short of the grace of God; lest any root of bitterness springing up cause trouble, and by this many become defiled;'

The wonder of God's personal providence was demonstrated from Psalm 138:8 'The LORD will perfect that which concerns me; Your mercy, O LORD, endures forever; do not forsake the works of Your hands.'

The importance of private prayer and church fellowship in the life of the believer were frequently touched upon, and the ongoing fight of faith and struggle for holiness clearly taught from passages such as 1 Timothy 6:12 'Fight the good fight of faith, lay hold on eternal life, to which you were also called and have confessed the good confession in the presence of many witnesses,' and Romans 7:24–25 'O wretched man that I am! Who will deliver me from this body of death? I thank God through Jesus Christ our Lord!

Preaching which God honoured

In a short space of time, the chapel which could hold 600 people, was filling up with large numbers. Herrick reported:

Preached at Helens Lane three times. Our congregation is evidently on the increase, afternoon attendance very good, evening overflowed. Enjoyed much liberty all day. Hope that I feel thankful to him who enables me to speak.

But it was usefulness in the Master's service that Herrick was striving for, not just numbers. You can detect the joy in his heart, in the summer of 1814 when he could report:

Sunday July 17. Preached at Helens Lane morning and afternoon. My morning sermon comforted many, I hear.

Sunday July 24. Preached at Helens Lane morning and afternoon and at Boxted in the evening. Heard more concerning the usefulness of my labours on last Lord's day. Blessed be God for any usefulness. Lord, make me increasedly useful to poor sinners.

The Lord began to save people under faithful preaching; 13 new members were added to the church during the first year of Herrick's pastorate. The first convert was a servant girl, Susan Bruce, who worked for Mr Walford. This is how Herrick described the news:

A young woman servant to Mr Walford upholsterer, called on me and informed me that she was deeply impressed by a sermon preached by me at Helens Lane on Lord's Day evening Jan 23 on 'thy testimonies are wonderful etc.' Almighty God, thou possessest all power in heaven and upon earth, do thou to exert thy power in behalf of this female. Strengthen her impressions, sanctify her soul. May she feel the power and enjoy the sweetness of the gospel and prove an ornament to the religion of the meek and lowly Jesus.

In July of 1814, Herrick had the joy of proposing this woman for church membership, at the same church meeting where his own wife was given the right hand of fellowship.

Another interesting case was that of Elizabeth Golding who had been admitted to Helens Lane in 1797 yet was no longer considered a member in Drake's short pastorate. Herrick describes the situation:

Mrs Golding, who was an awful backslider when I came here told me this day of her anxious desire to be restored to her place in the church from which she was expelled for irreligious practices and a total neglect of divine worship.

So, with sinners being converted, backsliders restored, and believers blessed, everything seemed to be set fair.

Carrying out pastoral duties

Herrick was a very hard-working pastor: assiduous in visiting the needy, thorough in preparing his sermons, careful in chairing church meetings and determined to make the best use of spare time available for reading. A few extracts from his diary give an idea of the ceaseless activity and the full range of his responsibilities. For November 28, 1814, he writes:

Visited Mrs Pennick, Manning, Simpson, Sarls, Daniels and Webb. Wrote to Mr J Douglas and the Rev. S Douglas by Mr Lester. Bought Seed's posthumous works and the *Spectator* for 14 shillings and 6 old books. Expounded in the evening at Helens Lane.

The people he visited were by no means all church members; they included interested listeners from the congregation and sometimes their sick relatives.

For December 2, 1814, he records:

Recomposed an outline on 'ye became followers of us etc.' Read 41st and 42nd sermons in Flavel's 'fountain of life.' I have now finished the volume. His style is plain and searching. Many allusions to ancient stories. Much piety and zeal. Several sentiments not in exact accordance with my own, such as more than half being damned etc. Yet on the whole it may be read with much advantage. Dined and drank tea with Mrs Thorn senior. Attended church meeting in the evening, one admitted, Mrs Simpson, called under my own ministry. Blessed be God for this and every encouragement. The Lord keep her from evil.

This first year was a period when the use of his gifts was expanding; he was becoming more well known in the towns around Colchester. In the summer, he preached at an anniversary service at Mersea by the seaside for the first time. He was on friendly terms with local Methodists and he spoke at the chapel in Ardley. In November, he spoke at a chapel in Bergholt, 11 miles to the north of Colchester. His normal procedure was to preach from an outline, but he was not rigid in this. On one occasion, he felt unable to speak with pleasure on the topic he had prepared; he says in his diary:

> I therefore chose another text in the vestry and though my first attempt in that way I enjoyed liberty.

Extempore preaching never became a habit; but it is interesting to see the flexibility of his mind and spirit.

We are not to think that everything he put his hand to in this first year was fruitful, although much prayer had been offered. In January 1815, he started a school with just 9 pupils. He found it so time consuming that he gave it up in April, with disastrous consequences, as we shall see in the next chapter. On June 12, 1814, he preached a sermon about God's personal providence, at Helens Lane. This was used in what seemed a remarkable way as the diary records:

> This evening Mr S Mansfield told me that he sent his servant this morning to invite Mr Waller to dine with him, who afterwards told him that this circumstance saved his life, for the distress had so overcome him as to lead him to prepare for self-murder. He apparently was actually prepared and a little longer would have completed the awful business. Mr M brought him to hear me in the morning, I preached on the providence of God, in which I

considered that there was a God, that he governed the world, that he sometimes permitted very trying providences to visit the best of men, that these were always intended to answer important ends. I considered the agency of God in giving us and in taking away our comforts and concluded with exhortation to resignation. The sermon was so appropriate that they were both much affected. It is remarkable that I was led to preach on this subject with considerable reluctance.

Herrick faithfully records in January 1815, however, that poor Richard Waller, at 79 years of age, took his own life in the end. It is not ours to judge, but the disappointment and sadness must have been harrowing.

Even though he was so young, Herrick faithfully challenged inconsistent Christian behaviour among professing believers, even in those much older than himself. He tells us of a problem with old Mrs Thorn. This lady, who had been under church ministry for 20 years, had developed the sinful habit of telling her servant to say she was out, when she was all the while at home.

To finish this chapter on a lighter note, we should record that Herrick was not an 'all work and no play' man. He enjoyed relaxing with his wife and friends, and some of his habits in this respect might disturb 21st century sensitivities. A morning spent fishing, walking in the country, or visiting the seaside would shock no one; neither would drinking tea with his family and friends; but to actually record it in his diary 910 times in 6 years does border on fixation! It was a relatively new drink, but he obviously enjoyed it immensely. Smoking a pipe is more controversial to modern Christians, but it seems to have been surprisingly common. The damage it does to health would have been completely unknown at the time; in fact, Herrick's very first mention of smoking was to describe its health benefits:

… visited Mrs King and smoked almost the whole afternoon for my cold. Think it did me good.

Most of the smoking was with his friends Lester, Baldrey and Foakes, but godly ministers such as Hyatt, Hyde, Merchant and Hunwick also joined him in the activity. There is no mention of it beyond 1817, and it may well have been a habit that was dropped, as was that of drinking alcohol:

July 8, 1814 … To drink *no more* spirits except *medicinally*.

To conclude: the first year of Herrick's ministry at Colchester was a happy one. Stable friendships were established, church fellowship was sweet, and the preaching gave lasting fruit. Underneath, however, there was a relatively small, but vocal group of malcontents whose influence had waned. No longer did the rich and the well-connected have the last say in what went on in the church. Ordinary working class converts, even servant girls, now had a place and a voice in church meetings. This was unheard of in class sensitive Colchester; a volcano was about to erupt, in more senses than one!

Chapter 6
Unitarian crisis at Helens Lane—1815 to 1816

The beginning of trouble

The first inkling of trouble at Helens Lane surfaced in March 1815. It appears that James Mansfield—for long a closet-Unitarian—was dissatisfied with Herrick's gospel ministry and was encouraging a group of like-minded people to meet separately for worship. A handful of these were church members, mainly it is presumed his own family, but also other malcontents within the congregation and some who were trustees. These people felt perfectly entitled to meet on their own in the church building. Rev. Yorick Smythies, the rector of St. Michaels Church in Colchester and of a church in Little Bentley in the country 11 miles east of the town, seems to have encouraged the group at the beginning: he like Mansfield was in his eighties. Herrick notes in the old church minute book:[81]

> This day on going to Meeting we found the gate and the door of the alley leading to the side of the meeting locked. On sending to the Rev. Yorick Smythies's house we found he had locked the door and gate and taken the keys with him to Bentley, on which account we were under necessity of breaking open both the gate and door.

In his diary he suggests this was done 'to incommode us.'

This incident was followed, only two days later, by concern over the behaviour of James Spurgeon. This man was a subscriber when Herrick first came to Colchester, but he had been warmly received into full church membership as early as the 2nd church meeting in June 1814. Now there was doubt concerning the consistency of his Christian life. Three church members were sent to discuss the situation with him; the unfortunate response they received is chronicled in Herrick's diary:

> Messrs Nash and Golding came in the evening to converse with J Spurgeon, but he did not come, but afterwards confessed he was at St. Peters church. We went down to his house, when and where he used us all, but myself in particular in the most insolent and unchristian manner.

Spurgeon had undoubtedly fallen under Mansfield's Unitarian influence, and It was this incident, and the way it was subsequently handled, which Mansfield used as an excuse for all-out war.

Mansfield ups the ante

It was not long after this that James Mansfield senior showed himself in his true colours. At the next church meeting, members were asked to agree a letter of dismission for Joseph Drake, the previous pastor who had now been invited to a ministry in Ridgewell, some 24 miles west of Colchester. When the topic was raised, Mansfield refused to add his signature to the letter. He became angry, claiming that Drake owed him money. Herrick promptly dismissed the meeting.[82]

Ever careful to establish the facts, Herrick wrote to Drake and records in his diary:

> Received a letter from Mr Drake which seems to satisfy myself and friends that Mr Mansfield's charge was only the effect of personal pique and not founded in truth.

With no change in Spurgeon's behaviour, the church proceeded to discipline him. A special church meeting was held on a Monday, rather than the normal Friday, because of the seriousness of the issues at stake. Twenty-four Church members were present at the meeting and not one of them supported Spurgeon in his behaviour or voted for him to stay as a member.[83]

It is evident, even at this early stage, that there was a group around Mansfield, giving him moral support in his opposition. They showed this by refusing to attend the special church meeting on April 10, 1815; they included James Mansfield, Mary Tillet, his housekeeper, Mary Wright his married daughter, and Mr and Mrs Baldrey, two of Herrick's close friends.

The opposition of the Baldreys reached a climax, two days after this church meeting. Herrick, apparently, had hired the Baldrey's son Samuel, to help him teach in the little school that he had started in January that year. The closure of the school on the 12th April, must have been a body blow to Samuel Baldrey as well as his parents. Very strong words were exchanged when Herrick met with them the same day. James Mansfield relates his version of the discussion in a vitriolic pamphlet which he wrote in 1817, explaining his version of events that led eventually to division in the church.[84]

Mr. Baldry being disappointed, and thinking himself and son unhandsomely treated, ventured to remonstrate with Mr. Herrick on his breaking the agreement between them. Mr. H. became warm, and passionately said, it was a downright lie. Mr. B. surprised at this conduct in one from whom he expected better things, replied, that he did not know till last week that he was under a Romish priest [referring to the Spurgeon excommunication—Ed.], but he would be under him no longer.

This turn of events shattered Herrick. Baldrey appears to have been quite violent in his abuse of Herrick when they met. To receive such treatment from one of his closest friends and to have his character vilified led to many tears, but the Lord comforted him when he attended the house of God.

To the stress of these personal differences was added financial worries at the end of March 1815. To add salt to the wound, Mansfield decided to reduce the quarterly payment Herrick received. The diary records:

> This morning Mrs Mary Tillet, housekeeper to Mr Mansfield my deacon, brought me 15 one-pound notes, in part of payment of my salary. It looks very strange. He has always brought it himself and never less than 25 pounds. However, I will take no notice of it at present.

This was quite extraordinary cruelty on Mansfield's part. He never admitted the charge of underpaying, but it did appear a deliberate attempt to unman his opponent.

The offending party excommunicated

Herrick knew that his opponents' real plan was to drive the gospel from the chapel. He did not charge them with this at the time; it would have been difficult to prove. But later he makes it abundantly clear. At the first church meeting in the new building, Herrick spoke of the problems they had had in the Old Meeting:[85]

> owing to the mixture of the disciples of Christ, with those who were the enemies of the cross ...

In the preface to his book Immanuel, Herrick is even more forthright about the motives of his enemies:[86]

In this place, the writer, on account of his warm attachment to the Gospel of God our Saviour, was abused, and treated in the most cruel manner, with a view to drive him away from the place in which providence had placed him for the defence of the gospel, to make way for men of sentiments more congenial to those of the trustees, though abhorred by the congregation, consisting of more than six hundred persons.

Herrick acted in the only way he felt he could—he treated the opposition as a matter for church discipline. By the end of June, 1815, all the offending members had been removed from church membership. First of all, he dealt with Mr and Mrs Baldrey:[87]

Our 14 Church meeting was held, when Mr James Nash was shown and appointed to be a Deacon of this church by the unanimous vote of the members.

Benjamin Baldrey and Phanuel his wife, were dismissed from this church, for inconsistent conduct. There were about 24 members present, and only one, viz, Mr Mansfield for them. He behaved in a very violent and abusive manner, but it had no effect.

A month later at the 15th church meeting, Mansfield and his party were dismissed:[88]

This was a special meeting called to consider the conduct of James Mansfield Senior Deacon, Mary Tillet and Mary Wright, when it was unanimously agreed that their conduct was highly inconsistent, and such as we could by no means tolerate. Mr M had abused his pastor, insulted the members, destroyed the harmony of the church, kept back part of the subscriptions etc, and the others had been concerned with him, and supported him in all his improper practices.

All suspended. There were present in all twenty-two. This evening also, Thomas Foakes was unanimously appointed assistant Deacon with Mr James Nash.

Sensibly, Herrick was strengthening the church leadership, by appointing two deacons to replace James Mansfield senior.

Effect on Herrick's mental state

It would have been surprising if Herrick could have taken all this intense aggravation without an effect on his health and well-being. He confesses in his diary that all the opposition had unhinged his mind. In particular:

Their threats and insults terrify me sometimes, so that I know not what to do.

The following day he inserted an earnest short prayer to his Lord and Master:

Almighty God, thou knowest the trials I have gone through, those I am in now and what are yet to come. Thou knowest my love to my dear people, and my desire to stay among them, if consistent with thy will I beseech thee to grant it. May we be directed to such steps as are calculated to promote peace. May we be delivered from our adversaries, may our trials be sanctified and may we be sweetened for glory. On our deliverance I do solemnly covenant with myself, that I will as near as may be, observe the day on which it took place, and keep a day of solemn thanksgiving in my own house; this will I do by the help of God. Signed: Joseph Herrick.

What had probably frightened him as much as anything, was

a letter he had received on June 6, 1815 from the supposed trustees. It is shown in its transcribed and original forms below:

We whose names are hereunder written, and being the majority of the trustees of the Meeting house in Bucklersbury Lane otherwise St. Helens Lane in Colchester, do hereby give you notice that from and after the twenty fourth day of June instant your services as preacher at such Meeting house will be dispensed with, And that from and after such time we shall consider you entitled to no part of the subscription or funds applicable to the payment of a Minister for the performance of Divine Service in such Meetinghouse. Dated the sixth day of June 1815.

To the Rev. Joseph Herrick

James Mansfield   Charles Heath
Isaac Brett   Thomas Inman
James Mansfield Junior
John Hubbard
James Buxton

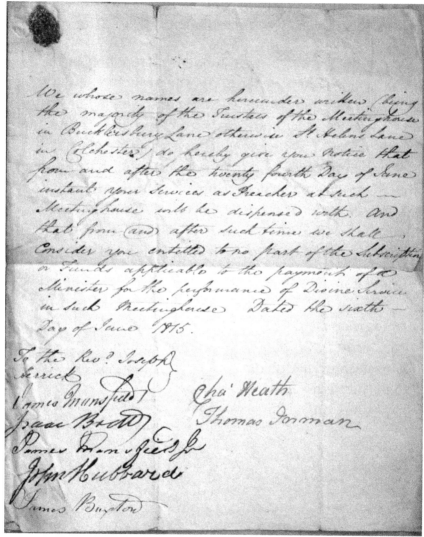

Figure 6: 'Trustees' dismissal letter to Herrick In June 1815

This letter, a full year before the unroofing of the chapel, was like a bolt from the blue—cutting him off from the church he loved, depriving him of his very livelihood. When he looked at it in the cold light of day, however, he could see how devious the 'trustees' had been.

Herrick was able to compare the letters' seven names with the entire list of those appointed in April 1800 under Isaac Taylor's pastorate, and with the group of men who resigned from the chapel in 1811 after welcoming John Church to the platform. The table below shows the comparison.

Trustees 1800	Resigned 1811	Supposed 1815
James Mansfield		James Mansfield
John Agnil		
Charles Heath	Charles Heath - Deacon	Charles Heath
James Thorn		
Henry Thorn		
James Buxton		James Buxton
John Hubbard	John Hubbard - Deacon	John Hubbard
Isaac Brett		Isaac Brett
James Mansfield Jr		James Mansfield Jr
David Lloyd		
William Bland		
James Walford		
Thomas Inman	Thomas Inman	Thomas Inman
Richard Golding		

Table 3: Old Meeting Room 'Trustees' 1800 - 1815

Three of the supposed 1815 trustees had supported the antinomian John Church in 1811, and then left the fellowship in chaos: Heath, Hubbard and Inman. The first two men claimed to be deacons at the time: this was not the case. What were they now doing as trustees, and how could their judgment be trusted? The seven who wrote were *not* a majority of the original 15, nor had they consulted with four of the trustees who were friends of Herrick: Thorn, Bland, Walford and Golding. The letter was a total sham. Future letters from the trustees were ignored or even sent back without being opened.

Overtures of peace

Herrick had prayed for peace, and he made many attempts to settle the differences between the church and Mansfield's party. Herrick asked advice from the ministers in his connection, including both his sponsor Thomas Wilson in London and his mentors John Thornton and Samuel Douglas. Agreement was finally reached: William Crathern, a local pastor at Dedham, and regarded as the father figure among Congregational ministers in the region, was asked and agreed to arbitrate. Mansfield's chief complaint was that Herrick had acted high-handedly and excluded well respected members for trivial reasons. Mansfield's comments are:[89]

> ... He proceeds upon these frivolous grounds to the last solemn act of power, that of separating a member from the body ... and ... all this too against persons of pious habits, and of irreproachable reputations, from whom he had received every hospitable attention, as well as other tokens of friendship ...

Numerous meetings were held between the parties, and Crathern suggested that the exclusion orders should be reversed. Mansfield in his pamphlet assures us that this did happen:[90]

... the result ... was, Mr M, Mrs Wright and Mrs Tillett were restored to their places in the church as having been unjustly suspended.

In the end, Mansfield and his party were so offended by their treatment that they claimed to have no wish to resume membership. Whether this was true, or a realisation that doctrinally the two groups could never meet in harmony, much as light cannot dwell with darkness, it is difficult to judge. What happened was that war was eventually resumed with increased intensity, every effort being made to make life for Herrick as uncomfortable as possible.

Preaching during a time of persecution

How does a minister react to criticism of his sermons and persecution of his person? There are numerous cases among the churches around Colchester where the minister resigned very soon after difficulties arose. It happened twice to the minister geographically closest to Herrick—John Savill. First, he resigned in 1828 from the Lion Walk Congregational church in Colchester; not many years later he left Halstead church too when he was unable to get the unanimous support of the members. A similar story could be told of John Fielding at Coggeshall and the Baptist minister at Eld Lane church in Colchester. Herrick was made of sterner stuff. He had no intention of resigning when he saw that truth and the large majority of listeners who loved it were very much on his side, but it took God-given courage and mental toughness to do it.

There is a distinct danger of ministers becoming paranoid when they are under fire. There is also the danger of overreacting and fighting fire with fire. The preacher is in a unique public position and can fall into the trap of making applications of the sermon which can only apply to some 'perceived enemy' in the congregation. Herrick fell into this trap a few times during the pressure of severe trial. He recorded in his diary that his preaching was very plain and faithful. Faithful preaching can be heavy preaching. Mansfield was the clear target of a sermon preached in March 1816, and the unfortunate recipient gives the details in his pamphlet:[91]

When the sermon commenced, his text was, 'And every plant that my heavenly Father hath not planted shall be rooted up.' 'For what purpose (said Mr. H.) are some of you here this morning? You are not come to worship God; sometimes you are here, and sometimes you are absent, you come because you will come, and then again you will keep away. Some there are who have been long standing in the church, who think they are of the people of God, that they have a right to be there because it is the place of their fathers. They have maintained an outward decent profession, done some good deeds, so are deceiving themselves; they are there, but nobody knows how they came there; like plants that are self-sown, at last discovered to be of no use, but obnoxious to the church of God, they must be cast out, they are not of my heavenly Father's planting. And these aged sinners go on as a French author expresses it, 'with frost in their bones and snow on their heads and go crawling to hell on all fours' ... some are come out of curiosity, but some are come here out of sincere attachment to me, to the cause of Christ, and the doctrines of the gospel which is preached within these walls. Some of you are come here to face your opponents, who desire to drive from you, if possible, that gospel which they hate, and to extirpate it from these walls. But, my friends, we have but to admire how your minds have been supported by the promises of the gospel, and I trust now and exhort you to stand firm to a man, and not to fret yourselves because of evil doers; they shall be cut down like grass at noon, and withered before it is evening, and we shall see our desire upon our enemies. Satan is always busy, always ready to stir up fellows of the baser sort to disturb the church of God.'

This was truthful, certainly, but far, far too strong.

The later part of this quote is very gentle by comparison to the comments about Mansfield and gives some idea of how Herrick dealt with church members who were true believers. His love for them, and his great desire to encourage them to hold fast to the faith comes across very strongly. This is typical of Herrick's preaching during the second year. The diary gives a detailed record of the Bible passages he preached from during the first two and a half years of his ministry. During the first year, Herrick preached two thirds of the time from the New Testament, much of the preaching being gospel oriented. In the year of the troubles, Herrick preached *nearly half the time* from the Old Testament, with more emphasis on *encouraging believers* to rely on the promises of God. Here are some examples of his sermons during these difficult times:

In April 1815

Trust in the Lord can banish fear: Psalms 56:11 'In God I have put my trust; I will not be afraid. What can man do to me?'

God promises to be present with believers in trial: Isaiah 43:2 'When you pass through the waters, I will be with you; and through the rivers, they shall not overflow you. When you walk through the fire, you shall not be burned, nor shall the flame scorch you.'

In May 1815

God will never forsake his people: 1 Samuel 12:22 'For the LORD will not forsake His people, for His great name's sake, because it has pleased the LORD to make you His people.'

In June 1815

Hope in God lifts the downcast: Psalms 42:5 'Why are you cast down, O my soul? And why are you disquieted within me? Hope in God, for I shall yet praise Him for the help of His countenance.'

In July 1815

God refines his people through trials: Job 23:10 'But He knows the way that I take; when He has tested me, I shall come forth as gold.'

In September 1815

God holds up those who fall: Psalms 145:14 'The LORD upholds all who fall and raises up all who are bowed down'.

When the trials reached their climax in February—April 2016, the preaching became even more personal and reassuring to the believers he cherished and wished to stand.

In February 1816

Those hated for Christ's sake will endure to the end: Mark 13:13 'And you will be hated by all for My name's sake. But he who endures to the end shall be saved.'

Builders for God will be given a sword for protection as well as a trowel to build: Nehemiah 4:17 'Those who built on the wall, and those who carried burdens, loaded themselves so that with one hand they worked at construction, and with the other held a weapon.'

In March 1816

God works all things for the Christian's eternal good: Romans 8:28 'And we know that all things work together for good to those who love God, to those who are the called according to His purpose.'

True believers have always been persecuted by unbelievers: Galatians 4:29 'But, as he who was born according to the flesh then persecuted him who was born according to the Spirit, even so it is now.'

In April 1816

Little strength leads to fainting in adversity: Proverbs 24:10 'If you faint in the day of adversity, your strength is small.'

The character of our enemies: Psalms 55:20 'He has put forth his hands against those who were at peace with him; He has broken his covenant.'

The lull before the storm

After restored church membership had been offered to the Unitarian party in Helens Lane, the last four months of 1815 were relatively free of incident. There was consternation, however, when James Nevill, one of the Unitarian party, stood up during a Sunday service in September to announce that Isaac Taylor, now a pastor in Ongar, Essex, was returning to take a funeral service for one of their number. This was arranged with little reference to Herrick or his deacons, and probably explains Herrick's rather dismissive comments of Taylor's 'ineffectual labours,' in his write-up of the history of the church in Helens Lane in the Stockwell Chapel minute book. Herrick and his friends still attempted to sort differences out with James Mansfield senior during these months, but nothing came of it, largely owing to Mansfield's stubbornness. Herrick was again disturbed to hear on 15th December 1815, that Mansfield intended to force him to leave the next day. Thankfully, the Lord answered his earnest prayers and he was able to preach the following day with much liberty and no interference. Herrick marvelled that he had managed to survive the malicious attempts of his enemies to get him out of his post.

With a thankful heart, New Year's Eve arrived and Herrick could say:

> I have now arrived at the close of that year which has been the most trying one of my life. But, bless the Lord, O my soul, for amidst trials in the family, the church and the world, God hath dealt bountifully with thee. May I on entering the new year, enter on a new course of life, a life of more faith on the Son of God, Amen.

Political, economic, and climatic conditions in 1816

Naturally speaking, 1816 was one of the worst years in which to have a church problem, especially in Colchester.

Politically, the country was on its knees. The battle of Waterloo in June 1815 had ended 23 long years of debilitating conflict—the French revolutionary wars, swiftly followed by the Napoleonic wars. Colchester was a city where soldiers were in barracks, as many as 7,000 at the height of the war with Napoleon. Weary, wounded and disaffected men were returning there during 1816, and the barracks were being decommissioned.

The weather in western Europe during 1816 was nothing

short of disastrous. It has been called the 'year without a summer.' The reasons for this were not understood at the time, but climatologists have done much research to uncover the underlying causes.[92]

A violent volcanic eruption of Tambora, in the East Indies (Sumbawa island / modern-day Indonesia) in April of 1815, threw enormous amounts of dust and sulphur dioxide into the stratosphere, which spread around the globe, not only preventing direct insolation (radiation from the sun Ed.), but leading to a distortion of the global wind circulation.

This eruption was so large, it was rated VEI-7 (Volcanic Eruption Index 7) and described as 'super-colossal'. Such an event would occur globally only every 500 to 1000 years, and it was 100 times more powerful than the eruption of Mount St Helens in 1980. Some 70,000 people in Indonesia are estimated to have lost their lives in the lava flow, tsunami and famine resulting from ash poisoning of the crops.[93]

In England in 1816, the average summer temperature was only 13.4C, some 2C lower than the average: among the two or three coldest summers ever recorded. Snow in Europe was a strange orange colour, and it was still falling in June. In Colchester, it snowed all day as late as April 14th, and further snow was seen on May 12th. If it was not snowing it was raining for much of the summer in Essex. So cold was it in the Lake District, that snow was seen on the slopes of Helvellyn on the 30 July, 1816.[94]

Although in Essex most of the wheat crop had been harvested by September, hail and frost had seriously affected potatoes, beans, peas and barley, and in parts of the county ice was four inches thick (in early September).

Some idea of the depressing effect of the perpetual greyness and constant rain can be felt from the first nine lines of Lord Byron's poem 'Darkness,' written when the poet was trapped with the Shelleys in Geneva in the summer of 1816:[95]

> I had a dream, which was not all a dream.
> The bright sun was extinguished, and the stars
> Did wander darkling in the eternal space,
> Rayless, and pathless, and the icy earth
> Swung blind and blackening in the moonless air;
> Morn came and went—and came, and brought no day,
> And men forgot their passions in the dread
> Of this their desolation; and all hearts
> Were chilled into a selfish prayer for light:

The summer of 1816 was so bad in Britain that many more people than normal emigrated to the USA. The poor weather devastated harvests throughout western Europe, leading to the worst famine of the 19th century. Britain was able to limit the food shortage by importing vast quantities of grain from North America, but the cost of this meant that bread prices in 1817/1818 more than doubled.[96]

Another concern in 1816 was the position of trade. Andrew Phillips describes the whole period from 1720 to 1830 in Colchester as 'The Long Decline.' The wool trade, once a staple of East Anglian industry, was in serious decline, the French wars putting a final nail in the coffin.[97] Amos describes the state of industry in Essex:[98]

> In the first half of the nineteenth century, Essex was a predominantly agricultural county. The rapidly dying woollen industry in the Braintree-Halstead area was replaced by silk manufacture, but the majority of Essex workers earned their living on the land. Small industries included straw-plaiting, salt manufacture, corn-milling,

brick-making, and the production of gunpowder.

Unemployment was a serious issue after the wars, and Essex was not without men who in their desperation would damage agricultural machinery or set fire to barns or haystacks to draw attention to their plight.

Hunger, unemployment, gloom and perpetual rain are a poor recipe for contentment. We should not be surprised that disaffection was openly expressed in Essex during 1816, even in a church situation.

One final comment needs to be made regarding James Mansfield. We have seen that this man was in the bay making trade. Baize is derived from coarse wool, and the woollen trade was in terminal decline because of the wars with France. By 1812, Mansfield was one of only three makers still in business, and we understand that he had closed down shortly afterwards.[99] Financial concern would have certainly influenced this business man's health and temper in 1816.

Build up to the final act

The first act of aggression from Mansfield's party in the new year took place on the last Sunday of January 1816. Samuel Mansfield took it upon himself to turn two church members out of the seat they were occupying, intending by this to indicate that the trustees had the right to decide who should occupy the pews. On February 2, a group of 'trustees', then took possession of the meeting room without warning either pastor or deacons. This was the first of eight such occasions from February to April when the Unitarian group treated the meeting room as if it belonged to them. They either decided to have a secret meeting of their own or came to disrupt a meeting in progress by evicting church members from their pews. Three of these incidents will give an idea of their tactics and the congregation's response.

On the morning of February 19, Herrick met Mansfield senior on the way to Helens Lane for a meeting. Mansfield was there with four of his supporters who obtained a workman to break open the church door. During the arguments that followed Herrick was roughly treated and his coat was torn.

The second incident was even more unseemly. The date was Tuesday April 2, 1816:

This evening, about 6 o'clock, Messrs Mansfield, S Mansfield, Podd, Brett, Nevill, Spurgeon, 2 Club's, Best, Henning junior, M Tillet, M Wright etc, assembled at our meeting house. Mr Nash and myself went, found them singing, when we began singing also, and this put a stop to the service. They abused me in the most shocking manner, their language too foul to be written. There were soon about 200 people there: our adversary decamped about dusk, hissed and hooted down the lane by the people. Saw the place clean and secure and then went to Rev. J Savill and spoke at the missionary society in much trepidation, but it vanished in speaking. Called on Mr Lester, found several friends there and two at home. Mr Bridge called and would give me ten shilling. 'O Lord, how very kind art thou to the unworthiest of thy servants!' Mr Simpson spent an hour with me. Was comforted by hearing from both the last named that Mr Savill seemed to commiserate my circumstances.

The Unitarian party was clearly growing bolder: five people on February 19 had grown to a group of more than 12 on April 2. The 200 spectators were probably not all church members, neither can we condone the hissing and hooting by Herrick's supporters—the situation was clearly out of control. The third example indicates a degree of riotous behaviour which was not unknown from unbelievers in 1816, but it is sad to see in a church building or anywhere. On April 9, there was a normal Tuesday lecture at Helens Lane to which three of Mansfield's party came. Herrick relates what happened in his diary:

At ½ past 4 went to meeting. The people kept coming until 6, when I began service by singing the 146th hymn in B & M, 18 verses. I then read the 37th Psalm, sang the same Psalm in Dr Watts, gave an exhortation and concluded with prayer and 'praise God from whom all blessings flow etc.' I then left the vestry and put on my hat to go, had our opponents (viz. S Mansfield, T Podd and J Nevill) retired, but as they continued in the vestry, a great number soon went in to them, and very soon there was a great uproar, hissing, clapping, laughing etc., but I could not distinguish anything that was said. I did not interfere in any way, but kept my seat in Mrs Lay's pew. After some time I heard that S Mansfield had retired, and soon after I saw Podd and Nevill come out, borne along by the violence of the crowd, who testified their displeasure in every way they could. Thus, they left the meeting house amidst the hisses and shouts of about 200 people. I then recommended the people to retire: they did, and the clerk locked the doors, the crowd going generally to the right, myself and a few others to the left. I walked up to the house of Mr Marsden in company with him etc. When we arrived in Culver Street, we heard shouting, which alarmed us. Mr M went to inquire into the cause and found that a great number of people had followed N and P and pelted them with mud to testify their indignation at their conduct. They repeatedly endeavoured to gain shelter in some friendly house, but were denied admittance, till arriving at the Cross Keys public house, they found temporary asylum from the infuriated mob, which by this time had very much increased. A great many went in to see their enemies covered with filth and afraid of venturing again into the streets, but the people were determined to have Nevill given up to them that they might escort him home, with those honours which he was even then pretty well laden, and therefore after long waiting he was again exposed to popular indignation and necessitated to make the best way a man in his circumstances could to his own house.

Not long after this troubling event, Herrick called a meeting of friends and ministers. After all the aggravation of 1816, Herrick was after good advice and a peaceful resolution with the Unitarian party. The consensus seemed to be that he would have to put up with his enemies meeting at his meeting house when they pleased. Herrick felt terribly discouraged; almost ready to give up. He went to the Lord, very much bowed down by his continued tribulation. He records his prayer:

O Lord, do thou regard thy creature. Suffer me not to be trodden down but deliver me for thy mercies' sake. O, deliver me in thine own way, which is always the best way. Take my troubles from me, or me from them, for Jesus Christ's sake, Amen.

How soon the Lord gave his servant reassurance:

Called at Lester's, found there had been no disturbance at the meeting, which I dreaded, but scarcely expected; Bless the Lord etc.

In all the trials he went through, Herrick was aware of the exhortation of the scriptures: 1 Timothy 4:16 'Take heed *to yourself* and to the doctrine. Continue in them, for in doing this you will save both yourself and those who hear you.' He wished to maintain the resolutions he had made at the start of his ministry in Grays, but one thing he had struggled with was getting up early enough to spend precious time with God. He could record in his diary for April 1, 1816:

I have been enabled 10 days to rise between 6 and 7 and hope I have now mastered myself in this matter.

Herrick and his friends continued to consult their lawyers as to the best way of resolving the dispute at Helens Lane. They examined the meeting house trust deeds; they even considered suggestions from Mansfield's lawyer:

Mr J Thorn and Mr J Rouse called concerning a mode of reference suggested by my opponents' lawyer and Mr Daniel. 'O Lord, direct me. Make my path plain because of my enemies.'

The next day was the Lord's Day: would the Unitarians behave any differently? Sadly not. Two of their party had the temerity to come and turn people out of their pews. A constable was summoned and the congregation hissed as they departed.

Because of Mansfield's party's aversion to talking things over with pastors or deacons, Herrick's friends suggested some form of arbitration involving laymen. Herrick himself was decidedly against this, but an unsuccessful attempt was made to go along this route. The whole of May 1816 went by without incident, in retrospect an ominous sign that a plot was being hatched. June 1, 1816 was Joseph and Ann's second wedding anniversary, and Herrick records in his diary:

This is the 2nd anniversary of my marriage, since which I have had many mercies and many sharp trials, but in the midst of all have had to bless the Lord. May we be married to Christ and live happily together in the enjoyment of his love, Amen … NB I have been at peace all last month and was promising myself repose, but this month is ushered in with a trial. They intend, I am told, unroofing the meeting house. 'O Lord, I am in thine hand. Do with me as seemeth good unto thee. Turn the counsel of my enemies into foolishness and establish my cause if consistent with thy will.

Within two day the unroofing of Helens Lane had begun, as described in Chapter 1—a truly astonishing resolution to the dispute; a final separation between two groups of people who could, in truth, never agree.

Assessment, conclusions, and lessons

It is not easy after 200 years to make a wholly accurate assessment of what happened in Helens Lane. Reading Mansfield's version of events is disturbing, especially as he claims it is based on an accurate journal of authentic evidence. In Mansfield's pamphlet he charges Herrick alone for being the cause of the division. In this document he makes four charges against Herrick, and I will attempt to assess each of them:

1. Unjustly excommunicating members for frivolous causes

There is no doubt that Herrick dealt very quickly with Spurgeon, Mansfield, Tillett and Wright. In none of the cases was a charge of heretical doctrine brought, though there is no doubt that Unitarian error was the real reason the church dismissed them. Herrick was very clear *after the event* that his enemies were 'Socinians' and 'enemies of the cross.' He was quite astute in early on identifying Mansfield as an enemy of the gospel. This was something that had been lost on Isaac Taylor, one of the earlier pastors. Herrick was also correct in assessing that those who sided with Mansfield had similar Unitarian views. The pity was that *he chose to exclude them for relatively minor offences*, rather than face up to the real problem and cut them off for heresy. Herrick made it abundantly clear in his preaching that Unitarian doctrine was the high road to hell. Mansfield admits as much, but protests loudly for freedom of judgment in doctrine:[100]

> The Roman Catholic cites the Scriptures in favour of transubstantiation; others again quote the Scriptures in favour of the Trinity. Are the Scriptures in both instances truly applied? Or is it right that a person who, after much patient and serious investigation, believes that they are both in gross error, who gives his reasons for his belief, invites discussion, one who has no purpose to serve but the honour of God, the promotion of truth and righteousness, and the happiness of men, should be answered or silenced by being consigned to perdition?

In Herrick's defence, we can say that after arbitration these four members *were* offered restored membership. None of them took it up, neither did they seek fellowship in another sound church in the area, choosing rather to create their own fellowship of non-Trinitarian worship. This shows very clearly that the division *was* about doctrine, and that Mansfield and his party *were* the aggressors, wanting Herrick out, and the chapel for their own use.

2. Falsely accusing the brethren

In church troubles, feelings run high. Accusations and counter-accusations fly from both sides; this happened in this dispute. Herrick as a young man barely out of his teens was put under enormous pressure. The Unitarian group harassed him continually, and there were times when irritation was shown, and strong words were exchanged. The thought of having his entire livelihood withdrawn by a small group of trustees must have been deeply disturbing. That he fell into name calling is regrettable, but not surprising in the circumstances. It is very much a case of the pot calling the kettle black. Mansfield's well written document is nothing short of scurrilous in its own name calling.

3. Preaching against identifiable persons

This highly regrettable characteristic of Herrick's ministry has been dealt with already. The brazen way, certain of the group positioned themselves in the Meeting house to discomfort him, must have exacerbated the problem. Nevertheless, this habit proves that, like all of us, he was a flawed individual, a sinner, but a sinner saved by grace. We have no way of knowing whether this was a feature of all his ministry, but despite his flaws, God used him for His glory.

4. Not always being truthful

The evidence presented by Mansfield is not very convincing. In any dispute like this, lying is the most common accusation from both sides. Under this heading, Mansfield raises the fact that Herrick ignored the regular notices which the trustees sent to him to quit the pastorship. But was it untruthful to ignore the dictatorship of a few unreliable men, when only one of the seven trustees was a church member?

The issue at stake was rule in the church. Mansfield's view could not be more unbiblical, involving as it did a small group of wealthy, socially superior trustees deciding who should be minister, how much he should earn, etc. This position was a carryover from the English Presbyterian view of church government, where leadership in the church was something which could be merited by pedigree, social position and wealth. There was nothing spiritual about it. Herrick's view was totally Biblical, involving elders/deacons with a full-time minister and a born-again membership. Decisions of membership and church discipline were agreed by members at a monthly church meeting: all members of either sex and whatever social class had a say in church affairs. This Congregational mode of church government never sat happily with Mansfield and his party, and most of the disagreements could be traced back to their wrong ideas as to how a church should be governed. It was not a case of 'priestly tyranny,' but Biblical discipline, applied without fear or favour.

Another thing that needs to be borne in mind is that the language used by both sides was much more extreme than would be considered normal in our relatively genteel 21st century. When Herrick was in the middle of his troubles, he made a detailed study of a dispute which had reached its climax in a local Independent church in Coggeshall, only 9 miles from Colchester. In that church, the deacons were in a protracted argument with Jeremiah Fielding the pastor. Their complaint was that his preaching was not feeding the flock, and that he was negligent in his pastoral visiting. Herrick records his assessment of the situation there in his diary:

Visited Mr Savill. Borrowed of him the answer to Fielding's letters. Read it 50 pages, but still I feel undecided and think he has been used ill in many things, though he has been very imprudent and much too warm. 'O Lord, keep me, and enable me to profit by the experience of others. Deliver me also out of all my troubles, through Jesus Christ, Amen.

Fielding, unwisely, had published two long and inflammatory

documents in his defence, adding up to more than 300 pages,[101] while the deacons had responded with a relatively mild publication of 65 pages.[102] An example of name calling from the first of Fielding's documents is almost comical in its extremity. Speaking of one of his deacons, Fielding asserted:

> His pride got quite insatiable and his ambition boundless … never human creature manifested a greater degree of haughty reserve and overbearing insolence …

In Herrick's dispute, we have only a 38-page document from Mansfield for public evidence. This derogatory document was published a year after Herrick had built the new church, and wisely he decided to publish nothing in reply. He merely confides in his diary:

> Read a book, price nine pence, written against me by the Socinians. Many things exceedingly false. Lord make the wrath of man to praise thee.

Herrick's alleged language is almost mild by comparison, though by a scriptural standard we can only deplore all malicious speaking: 2 Timothy 2:24 '… a servant of the Lord must not quarrel but be gentle to all, able to teach, patient.' We need constantly to be reminded that 'the tongue is a fire, a world of iniquity:' James 3:6.

As far as Helens Lane was concerned, we can be sure that God was guiding the outcome by his mysterious Providence. The unroofing of the Meeting Room led to a necessary separation, as the Scriptures make plain, 2 Corinthians 6:14–17: "Do not be unequally yoked together with unbelievers. For what fellowship has righteousness with lawlessness? And what communion has light with darkness? 15: And what accord has Christ with Belial? Or what part has a believer with an unbeliever? 16: And what agreement has the temple of God with idols? For you are the temple of the living God. As God has said: 'I will dwell in them and walk among them. I will be their God, and they shall be my people.' 17: Therefore 'come out from among them and be separate, says the Lord...

The true believers at Helens Lane were finally separated from the ungodly Unitarians who had blighted the church for decades. The unroofing, though highly inconvenient at the time, was God's providential hand of blessing on his true people. We shall see in the next chapter how things turned around.

Chapter 7
New Helens Lane history until it became Stockwell Chapel

The loss of the meeting house was a great shock to everyone, it was the talk of the town for days. Mansfield had the temerity, during this time, to try and influence people to deny Herrick any further preaching opportunities. Herrick's diary records:

> Was informed by Messrs Thorn and Walford that old Mansfield had been to Mr Daniels to solicit his influence to prevent my preaching at Mr Savill's. He wept and talked of his respectability and said everyone knows I (Mr Mansfield Ed.) am a good character, and now is the time for the Dissenters to support me! Amazing hardness and blindness! NB this convinces me they begin to feel uneasy.

In fact, Savill's church officers very kindly offered the use of their chapel on Sunday evenings. They wanted Herrick to understand, however, that they did it because of the distress he and his church were in: they were not taking sides in the dispute. This is an interesting comment on their part and gives an indication of how ineffectual Christians of the day were in dealing with Unitarians. The decades of debate over the Trinitarian issue, and the aggressive stance taken by Unitarians, made many Christians timid over a vital issue of doctrine. It was quite normal to treat them as fellow Dissenters: Christians with a slightly different perspective on a 'secondary issue!' It took a man of Herrick's bravery to shake people out of their harmful complacency.

Within a week of the unroofing, Herrick was back into his routine of sermon preparation, preaching to crowded congregations at Mr Savill's place in Lion Walk and at the gift houses. He decided that if he had no meeting room of his own then his own parlour at home would be fitted out for the purpose. Only nine days after the event he records that he had preached at home in the evening, and there had been a good attendance.

Love for his people and lost sinners compelled him to make every effort to continue against the odds.

God's providence in showing the way forward

Herrick's mind and heart were troubled by a host of conflicting questions in determining the way forward. Should he stay in Colchester, or should he take the unroofing as guidance that he should leave the town? If he stayed, would his congregation be for ever harassed by the Unitarians? If he remained, how would he be supported financially? If he stopped in Colchester, how could he manage without a building? If he built, where would that be and how would the expense be met? The most urgent questions that vexed him were: how could the needs of his flock be met if he left? Where would they go? Who would supply their needs? These issues were a regular matter of prayer in the month of June for the Lord to make his way plain. On the last day of June, he confided that he did not expect to be another month in the town.

He asked advice, both of his Colchester friends and his ministerial colleagues in Essex and London. Just at the point when his London friends were advising him to leave, the Lord encouraged his servant with some great kindnesses.

First there was the warm friendship of Thomas Marsden, the printer, who had large premises in Culver Street, right in the centre of town. He offered the use of his place for a regular prayer meeting for the first 14 months after their ejection from Helens Lane. This dear man was a widower, yet he opened his home to Ann and Joseph at a critical time, often invited them for meals, transported them when necessary and got fully involved whenever he could help. The first Sunday meeting they had at Marsden's house was a very special one, as Herrick records:

Preached at home morning and afternoon. Had a delightful meeting at Mr Marsden's in the evening. Surely God was with us.

The second thing Herrick could praise God for was the kindness of Christian people from a variety of occupations, not all in the Congregational denomination. A month after the unroofing of the chapel, when his personal money would have been running low, he lists some of the people who helped him:

Mrs Barns sent for me at 3 o'clock, went, was astonished when she told me that four or five of her friends had given her the following sums for me: Rev. W Marsh, vicar of St Peters £5, Mrs Austin £5, Mrs Barns etc. £2, others £1. How amazing! Church people are kind to a poor dissenting minister, kind and liberal, and that without solicitation. 'Great God, this came like every other mercy, from thy kind hand. Blessed be thy name for evermore, Amen and Amen.' Whilst recording the above mercy, another was received from an unknown friend, viz. A very handsome straw bonnet for Mrs H and a note for me with £2. 'O Lord, I am loaded with thy benefits. My table is spread in the face of my enemies. May thy kindness teach me to look to thee and depend upon thee.'

The third providence was the generosity of his friends in raising money for his support, and for possible building, only three days after his London friends had advised him to leave Colchester. They had a meeting on July 11, 1816 and between them offered the sum of £113—equivalent to a year's salary for a minister, in today's money. Many of them then visited Ann and Joseph to convey their prayerful support and interest.

Weighed against these positive providences was the constant worry about his people. This was such a heavy burden that on the last Monday of July, after preaching to them in the parlour at home on the Sunday, he confessed in his diary:

> This day I made up my mind to leave Colchester, and that for the following reasons. My people, though affectionate, are very poor. I dread because of that and the difficulty of the times. I do not think I should be comfortably supported. We have no men to take the responsibility, very few of real piety, none fit for deacons, only 6 men members. Some of the people who would expect to be at the head of the society are versatile, uncertain and dogmatical. Mr Savill is going to enlarge, Mr Marsh (vicar of St Peters Ed.) has done so, but little money to be got in the town. Wearied and disgusted with what I have here met with. Party spirit runs very high. Expect an addition to my family. Rev. S.D. advises me not to build. Think if I had another place my enemies would always annoy me. Fear that if any difficulties occurred, my friends would not be firm and that I should be upbraided for leading them into trouble and expense. Have prayed for divine direction, that the Lord would cross my will, if I will what is wrong. Still feel disposed to leave. Mr Wilson offers to send me to Banbury. Pray that I am not to go unless it be the will of God. Nothing appears to prevent it.

When he went to preach to his people that same evening he had a sorry tale to tell, but their reaction changed everything:

My mind much exercised about leaving my people. Expounded in the evening. Told my people that though I this night began the 38th Psalm, I had no hope of staying with them to finished. Many sighs and tears. Some of them stayed and spoke to me. Others were so much affected they moved slowly and silently away in great uneasiness. Would to God I could stay with them with comfort! His will be done.

After such a loving response, Herrick's mind was made up. Not for one moment after this was there any doubt that staying was God's will for him and his people. A mere four days later: August 2, 1816, a promising site for the new church came on the market. He and Messrs Rouse and Nash visited Jackson's warehouse at the corner of Helens Lane and East Stockwell Street, only 50 yards from the unroofed meeting room. They purchased it, had the land cleared, and building work was begun in earnest. The final seal of the Lord's approval came when he visited Thomas Wilson, his childhood mentor in London. Wilson thought it was Herrick's duty to stay and gave him £20 towards the building fund.

Exhausting work in building and begging for finance

The next three months particularly were filled with exhausting but exhilarating toil for Herrick. Dissenting ministers were renowned for the efforts they had to make to raise money to finance chapel building. Established churches had a good living; Dissenters like Herrick were left to raise money themselves. Not once did Herrick complain about doing what he could consider degrading work. Many of the local towns and villages around Colchester were visited day after day. The list is impressive: Boxted, Wix, Harwich, Manningtree, Witham,

Chelmsford, Coggeshall, Stisted, Braintree, Bocking, Finchingfield, Ardley and Ipswich. He preached in London too, and gathered impressive amounts of money there and in Tonbridge in Kent as well. All this had to be done while he kept up his preaching engagements. The diary for August 12, 1816 records the sort of tiring routine he had to endure:

Begging all day, good success. Expounded at home in the evening, after which a meeting at Mr Rouse's.

If he was not begging, then he was at the meeting, organising the building work. This was so worthwhile when the building was nearly completed and could be used, even if the roof was not finished and umbrellas had to be raised. With prayer, he records in October 1816:

Preached morning and afternoon in my new meeting, well attended, afternoon more than full. This is the first time of preaching there. O that I may be spared to see the cause flourish and be made instrumental in converting many to God.

In the space of only four months, the new chapel was built, and was opened officially on 13th November, 1816—a quite remarkable rate of progress. The opening is recorded in his 'Brief Historical Sketch':

Two sermons were preached, that in the morning by Rev. R Stodhart, of London, from 'Other foundation can no man lay than that is laid, Jesus Christ,' and that in the evening by Rev. J Thornton, of Billericay, from, 'O Lord, I beseech Thee, send now prosperity.' Many other ministers were present, and a crowded congregation contributed liberally to the help of the minister and his friends.

Among the ministers that day were Rev. William Crathern, the father figure from Dedham, and Rev. Jeremiah Fielding, who had had so much trouble when he was at Coggeshall. The collection amounted to a healthy £26–16–3¼.

Herrick ended 1816, the most eventful year of his life, with a prayer:

> May God sanctify all I have passed through and forgive all my unfruitfulness and if spared another year, make me more humble, holy and diligent, studious, zealous and believing for the sake of his dear Son, Jesus Christ, Amen.

New rules for a new church

After all the traumas of 1815 and 1816, Herrick gave much thought to the government of the new church. Here are a few of the features of the worship that was conducted in the new Helens Lane Meeting room.

The very first point Herrick makes is that church membership is 'for those who worship the Father, the Son and the Holy Spirit.' Trinitarian worship was essential, as he records:[103]

> ... we took into serious consideration the disadvantage we were under in our former connection, owing to the mixture of the disciples of Christ, with those who were the enemies of the cross, and therefore it was deemed expedient at the outset to provide against future trouble and inconvenience, by adopting such rules for the regulation of our conduct in church affairs, as would tend to the exclusion of heterodoxy, and the peace of the church, not only in our time, but in future days.

The rules adopted for government of the church were:

> We, the members of the Church of Christ, Helens Lane, Colchester, solemnly covenant and agree, before God, and

each other, that this Church be denominated, the Protestant Independent Church of Christ, assembling in Helens Lane, Colchester.

2. That this Church holds itself a true Church of Christ, independent of all other churches, capable of legislating for itself, and determines to acknowledge none but Christ for its head—to walk by his word—and to settle all its affairs by suffrage.

3. That all persons wishing for Communion with this Church shall apply to the Minister or Deacons, who shall represent the same at the next Church meeting, to the members assembled, when the Minister shall appoint the Deacons (or if there be but one, the Deacon and one other member) to converse with them, and direct them to furnish the Minister with some account of their Religious Experience by the next Church Meeting, when their Experience shall be read and the report of the Visitors received, after which the matter shall be put to the show of hands, and on a majority appearing for the person proposed, they shall be admitted by receiving the right hand of fellowship.

4. That no person shall be admitted a member of this Church without the consent of the Minister, and a majority of the Members.

5. That no person shall be admitted a Member of this Church who does not firmly believe in the Divinity of Christ, and entirely rely on the Atonement of the Lord Jesus Christ, and who does not receive the Holy Scriptures as a rule of life and manifest their conformity to them by a suitable conversation and conduct.

6. That if any Member walk disorderly, they shall be

admonished by a person appointed by the Church. If no good results from the first admonition, a second shall be given, by another person, appointed by the church. If no good results from this, the Minister shall visit them (if practicable) and on no beneficial effect appearing, they shall be summoned before the Church, to answer to them for their improper conduct, and shall be censured, suspended or excluded, as the church may think fit.

7. That the Lord's Supper be administered (if possible) on the first Lord's day in every calendar month, when every member shall attend unless prevented by illness, or something which may enable them to answer before the Church for their absence, and before the Lord Jesus Christ, at his coming.

8. That a meeting of the members of the Church be held on the Friday before the first Sabbath evening in every month, at 7 o'clock in the evening, to transact the business of the society, to admit or exclude Members, such Meetings to begin with singing and prayer, and to conclude in the same way if there be time, and to conclude by a short petition and benediction.

9. That Members of other Churches wishing for occasional Communion with us, shall produce a letter from the Churches to which they belong, testifying their real godliness and general consistency of conduct, and on such recommendation, shall be admitted.

Done at our Church Meeting

This 6 Day of Dec 1816

And signed at request of the Church

By us: Joseph Herrick—Pastor

James Nash—Deacon

Rule 5 is a clear doctrinal point, based on the bitter experience of having a vociferous Unitarian element within the membership in previous years. Never again would the church tolerate such a situation. Rule 6 shows the application of church discipline in an entirely scriptural way: first and second admonition of the miscreant, followed, in the case of no repentance, by a summons to appear before the gathered church as described in Matthew 18:17.

Continual enlargement of the church building

The early years up to the 1830s were years of faithful preaching and growth of church membership. The unity of doctrine made a big difference to the spiritual health of the church, and this was a cause of much thankfulness.[104]

A superficial measure of the church growth was the number of times the building had to be modified in the first 20 years after its initial construction. The building opened in November 1816 had no gallery, but in June 1817 a Christian friend offered an initial £20 for one to be built, as well as loaning the remaining money needed for three or four years. By the end of July 1817, a gallery had been constructed—a remarkably rapid build by modern standards. By 1821, 61 new church members had been admitted, and the chapel was regularly occupied with 600 or more in the congregation. Further enlargement was undertaken in 1824, and the special service to praise God for this took place, as recorded in the church minute book:[105]

September 8th 1824

Rev. John Hyatt preached two sermons on occasion of our enlargement of the Meeting House, on John 16:14–16, and 1 Cor, 6:9–11. Several other Ministers took the devotional services. The day was very pleasant, and I hope will long be remembered for its holy impressions. The collections amounted to 40..18..4 ¾. Our collections among ourselves to about 250..0..0. The whole of the undertaking will cost nearly £500.

By 1834 the chapel was showing signs of serious decay. The building had been made from rather poor materials, the foundations were not what they ought to have been, and significant subsidence had occurred. This had led to criticism which Herrick found disheartening, especially at a time when membership was growing fast and the pews were almost bursting at the seams. Herrick, in disconsolate mood, shared his thoughts in a letter to Thomas Wilson, in London:[106]

Letter to Thos Wilson Esq Congregational Library Bloomfield St Finsbury London April 30, 1834

Colchester, April 30, 1834

Dear Hon'd Sir,

When talking with you a few days since, in Town, about a new place of worship, you said—The place you occupy is a disgrace to the town, and I would tell them, were I in your place, that if they would not erect a new one I would leave.

I am not superstitious, but really, I feared at the moment, and told my family afterwards, that perhaps your words might prove prophetic.

Last evening the congregation was called together, by notice given on Sunday, to deliberate and decide on so important a matter. The meeting was small. Many of the most able to help absent, and very few zealous among those who were present. It seems very doubtful whether we shall accomplish it—and if not, my usefulness here will, I fear, be greatly impeded, for a settlement in the building has given some a notion of its insecurity, and this is made the most of by rivals and secret adversaries to the cause and so I feel therefore downhearted—and having always looked up to you from a boy, I could not refrain from writing to you, that you may not be surprised if circumstances should ultimately lead me to seek usefulness elsewhere, which would be hard with a growing church, and numerous applications for seats.

I beg you not to communicate what I have imparted in the anxiety of my heart, while I hope you will be so kind as to have an eye upon any place where there is an opening, and where you may think such poor endeavours as mine might be useful, should Providence permit me to leave here.

Those most zealous were very grateful for your kind offer of £50. But our senior Deacon is totally against removal, and indeed any great expense, and so I fear are the majority, fearing it might in the end cost them a good deal.

In the course of a week or two we shall be better able to decide—as it was determined to make private application to individuals, and then to meet and cast up the amount promised on the papers of the persons who have undertaken to go around. If a £1000 is subscribed I have said, we will venture—but I have little hope of such a sum, which would be but half of what is wanted, if so much.

With all good wishes, and desiring the aid of your counsels, and an interest in your prayers,

I am,

With very greatest respect,

Yours sincerely,

Jos^h Herrick

NB What makes our case additionally discouraging is, that both the Baptists and the Methodists are collecting for new places at this very time—just as if all the Dissenting places had got out of order at one time.

Herrick did not leave Colchester! He recovered from his low spirits and, sensibly, took both short and long-term measures to solve his building problems. In view of the opposition to substantial cost he immediately set in hand necessary strengthening work on the structure as it was. Within a month of this letter he recorded in the church minute book that the Meeting House was going to be thoroughly repaired, cleaned and decorated at a cost of just £60.[107]

Herrick continued to look for ways to enlarge the chapel in the longer term. A remarkable providence led them to purchase land adjoining the chapel. Herrick informed Wilson of what had happened:[108]

… the Proprietor of an old building and a piece of ground, adjoining our Meeting House, and nearly of the same size and form, returned from India, and gave us the refusal of it. He formerly asked £400, but as he is now about settling at Java, he let us have it for £270.

Donors came forward with the promise of money, upwards of £1100 was raised along with Wilson's promised £50. Building was carried out from May to October 1836, and Stockwell Chapel as it was called from then on was opened with great thankfulness on October 2, 1836. A full account of that great day is described by Herrick himself:[109]

Stockwell Chapel

Our place is now called, since the front has been turned into East Stockwell St. It was reopened for Divine Worship, after being closed ever since May last, on Tuesday Oct 4, 1836.

Two sermons were preached on the Occasion, by Rev. James Stratton, of Paddington, and Rev. Cas. Sherman of Surrey Chapel. More than 50 guineas were collected after each sermon. Morning comfortably full, Evening excessively crowded. About sixty dined together at the Lion. It was a very pleasant day throughout. May it be long remembered! And may the prayers then preferred continue to be answered for many years to come!

The expense of the undertaking has been upwards of £1000. Upwards of £1100 were raised before this day. The excellent Collections, and £50 from Mr Wilson, leave only between £300 and £400 to be raised hereafter to clear off the debt.

It is wonderful that this Christian Society should have existed and prospered as it has done. When the present Minister came, it was in a very low state, only 4 male and 7 aged female members. Mr Herrick also met with innumerable difficulties from Socinian Trustees, worldly opponents of the Cause, but after all the Cause has prospered, a noble Chapel is erected, a large congregation gathered, and a Church of between 2 and 3 hundred members! It was difficult for Mr H. on this delightful day to keep his eyes dry, the tear induced by grateful emotion was frequently starting.

Surely it shall be said at this time, comparing the present with the past, O Lord! Forsake not the work of thine own hands!'

Figure 7: Stockwell Chapel In 2015, now called Herrick House

Figure 8: Looking down East Stockwell Street from the chapel

The last word about this occasion will go to George Savill, the eldest son of John Savill, and at the time the mayor of

Colchester:[110]

The progress of this persecuted congregation is honourable to the perseverance of their pastor and to the fidelity of his people.

Lives changed by the gospel

The expansion of the church membership from 11 to around 250 in the course of 20 years is testimony to God's blessing on a gospel centred ministry. Examples of lives changed by the gospel will now be given.

William Carey was one of Herrick's very earliest converts, called under his ministry in March 1815. He plucked up courage to visit the pastor in October of 1815 and was so grateful for Herrick's help that he gave him a gift of a hare later that month. In spite of all Unitarian problems at the time, Carey is mentioned in the diary again in June 1816, when the old church was unroofed, and gave a donation of one dollar. Giving is a good sign of a changed and thankful heart. Carey and two friends visited Herrick shortly after the opening of the new building. Herrick recorded in his diary in December 1816:

Was much encouraged by a visit from Messrs Carey, Vincent and Jennings, all apparently, as according to their own confession, converted under my preaching. To God be all the glory. And O that they may be kept by him from falling away. May they keep decided and humble and grow in grace and prove a comfort to us and an honour to the gospel.

Carey was the first man to be received into fellowship in the new building in February 1817, there being, according to the church minute book, clear evidence of a changed heart. What a joy it must have been 27 years later when his wife was also received into church membership! Living as a Christian before his wife, and fervent prayer for her had been rewarded.

Mrs Baker was proposed for membership in December 1825, but strangely, withdrew her name at the next church meeting. Some very interesting news was then relayed to the meeting the following March.[111]

> Mrs Baker, who withdrew her name in Dec, owing to violent opposition from her husband, was this evening re-proposed, it having pleased God (apparently) to work a most marvellous alteration in her husband, who now attends all opportunities as constantly as herself.

This woman was gladly received into fellowship in May 1826, but we hear nothing more of her husband and can only assume that there was no real work of grace in his heart. Things started to go seriously wrong with Mrs Baker in 1832. The minute book records:[112]

> Mrs Baker's case, who has acted in a way that renders her religion altogether questionable, was left with the elders, to deal with as they please, and if they deem it proper after another month, to propose her erasure from the list of members' names.

Sadly, the elders found her case to be as bad as they had originally thought; so evil a person was she that her life was a disgrace to the church. She had to be excommunicated. But our God is able to restore the prodigal from wandering, and He did so wonderfully in the case of Mrs Baker. Six years later the minute book recorded:[113]

> Mrs Baker, who fell away for several years, was, after 4 or 5 months' consideration, and enquiry, restored. She seems to feel correctly—may it ever so appear!

Jacob Dennis's case is a heart-warming one, and a letter from him to Herrick survives among family memorabilia:[114]

Colchester September 29th, 1825

Reverend Sir. The several addresses and appeals you have lately made to us on decision of character, have made considerable impression on my mind. I believe that I am verily guilty in halting so long between two opinions. I hope and trust that God has done something for my soul. It will of course be required that I give a reason for that hope. I thank God, I trust devoutly, that from my earliest years I have been blest with a tender conscience and restrained from the grosser acts of iniquity, but I was a stranger to prayer, until a few years ago that I was seized with a violent palpitation of the heart. I thought that my life was going from me and expected that in a few minutes I should be launched into eternity. At that moment, the Lord was graciously pleased to shew me the exceeding sinfulness of sin and inspire me with hope in his mercy. I prayed earnestly that the Lord would grant me an assurance of my interest in Jesus Christ, this was all my desire. I did not ask to have my life spared, nor did I desire it, my hatred to sin was so great that I feared hell.

I bless God that he has not suffered me to give up secret prayer. It has pleased Him to spare my life and to exercise me with many trials, which I desire to consider as so many mercies as they have been the means of teaching me the value of a Throne of grace. I have no worldly motives in wishing to become a member of your church. Sin is my plague, the sincere followers of Christ I love, the house and service of God are my delight, and yet I exceedingly fear to enter into this solemn engagement with God. I linger on the plains and require to be hastened by a supernatural power.

Should I be admitted into Church fellowship I beg that God will pour down upon me the sanctifying influence of his Holy Spirit, that I may behold sin with increasing deformity and Jesus Christ with increasing beauty and be kept from bringing disgrace upon the Christian Name.

I am Sir, with the greatest respect

your obedient, humble servant,

Jacob Dennis

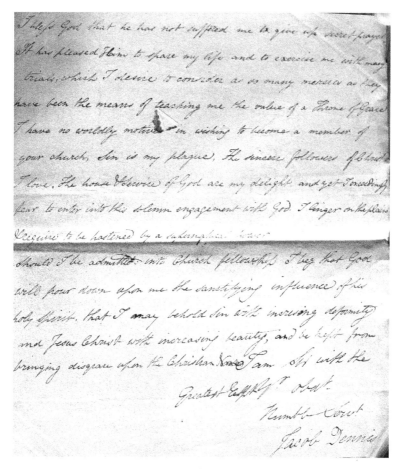

Figure 9: Part of letter from Jacob Dennis to Herrick in 1825

The marks of a true Christian believer are very evident in this humble writing, and Jacob Dennis was gladly and unanimously received into church membership in November 1825. The last page of his letter in its original format is shown in Figure 9 above.

Mrs Mason was converted under Herrick's ministry, and became a church member in January 1827. Too soon, she drifted away from the Lord and was not seen at Helens Lane. Here is her remarkable letter to Herrick some six years later, found among family memorabilia (spelling uncorrected, lines which could not be deciphered omitted):

Reverend Sir,

Feeling a great desire to return to the church again, I am quite willing to acknowledge my self rong in leaving in the way I did and can assure you, sir, I have suffered from that time to the present moment what I am not able to express. I have been like Noah's dove could not find any resting place, my dear Lord shut me up in dark dispare and I have cried, but with David hath the Lord cast off forever, will he be favourable no more, hath he in anger shut up his tender mercy from me—I have falling by iniquity, restore unto me the joys of thy salvation. I have been much comforted lately by these words—my grace is sufficient for thee my strength shall be made perfect in thy weakness. Lord I am week, but thou art strong, hold me by thy powerful hand. I must still hang upon him for he is precious to my soul ... I feel I must be decided. Dear Sir, pray for me that the Lord would make my soul sinssear and preserve me by allmighty power. I hope this will be a warning voice to any who may think of doing as I have ... (I) no sooner left the church than the Lord left me to see the depravity of my wicked heart ... Dear Sir this text I heard you preach from some years back and since this circumstance took place it has been very much imprest upon my mind to the benefit of my soul, for the Lord hath led me to turn again and look with my depraved heart and to see the determination and wickedness there is in it, yet I will still pray him because he hath by this led me to see my own weekness and his Allmighty power. His arm is not shortened that he cannot save neither is his ear heavy that he cannot hear. In him will I trust and not be affraid for he has sed return ye backsliding children for I am married unto you. I cannot give up my hope, how can I sink with such a prop as bears the world and all things up. Lord do with me as seameth good in thy site, so it may be for thy glory and my everlasting good. Dear Sir, I have never lost sight of you as being my spiritual Father. You sir, were the first instrument in the Lord's hands of bringing me to see myself by nature and my nead of a Saviour. May the Lord be ever with you and prosper you in your arduous labours. Whatever may you think best I am willing to comply with however I may feel prove it a word or two from you Sir would be most thankfully reseved if it is not asking too much as I should be very glad to know your mind as it would be a great relief to me,

your humble and obliged servant

M A Mason

Thursday evening

January 27

Mrs Mason was welcomed back into church fellowship with open arms. There are many tantalising references in the minute book to other, very interesting conversion stories, but these gems are the only ones where substantial information remains. They are sufficient to demonstrate the reality of the change the gospel produced, and the character of the preacher at Helens Lane.

Chapter 8
Herrick's early family life during times of trial

We have already indicated in the first chapter that Herrick's experience during the Unitarian crisis was character defining and character refining. We shall now go into more detail of how he was affected during and shortly after this period of heavy trial.

Joseph and Ann Herrick had a total of seven children born to them. Only two of these survived to adulthood: Ann and John Douglas. The details are shown below.

1. Ann, 16/04/1815–11/08/1815, died aged 4 months,

2. Joseph, 11/09/1816–27/10/1816, died aged 1 month,

3. Ann Douglas, 28/10/1818—married twice but died childless at an unknown date, in adulthood,

4. Joseph Archibald Douglas, 29/01/1821—died in his mid-twenties,

5. John Douglas 14/01/1823, died in 1884,

6. Douglas, born in 1828, died in the same year,

7. Douglas, 27/06/1830–20/11/1873.

The list tells a sad tale: three children died in infancy, one died in youth or slightly beyond; Douglas, the last child in the list, was born mentally and physically handicapped.

The death of their eldest two children—its effect on Ann and Joseph

Herrick gives a full account of the births and deaths of the first two children in his diary, with much briefer comments about the birth of Ann Douglas. We have seen that Herrick often worried about his wife's health, and the reason for this became abundantly clear during the two pregnancies he described in detail. During the first of these, there is frequent reference to Ann feeling unwell, fainting frequently, even being so ill that Joseph expected her to die before her full term.

In both pregnancies, Ann travelled to stay with her mother in London for a month, and this was a great help. Herrick recorded his delight at the birth of their first child:

... Went to the morning prayer meeting, when I came home found my wife safely delivered of a daughter. We expected a dreadful time, but God in mercy disappointed our fears. She had a very easy time; we have much reason to call on our souls and all within us to bless the Lord ... Mrs Lester was with my wife all the morning and evening. Mr L spent the evening with me. Wrote to Mr J Douglas.

Before baby Ann was eight weeks old serious illness set in, no medical treatment worked, simple things like fresh June air were no help either. Just before she was four months old Herrick recorded her sad demise:

This night, just before the clock struck 10, my dear babe expired without a sigh or a groan. Our mind very much affected by the scene. May the Lord sanctify it to our souls. Mrs Lester was here; she therefore slept with Mrs H and I sat with the child.

All this was happening just at the time when the Unitarian party was beginning to create trouble at Helens Lane. There is no doubt that the worry of having a sick wife added to the burden of the trials. This was even more the case during the second pregnancy from January to September 1816, when the Mansfield party increased their opposition. Ann was even more ill during this second period; in fact, there is good reason to believe that her mind was affected, and she acted quite out of character towards the end of her pregnancy. To add to this, their second child was born prematurely and lived in very poor health for only six weeks. So, we have the scenario: when Herrick's own mind is nearly unhinged by the severity of his church trials, his wife is unable to be any comfort to him as she is seriously damaged by an unusually troublesome pregnancy and a very sick child: a truly toxic tornado of trials. At this point sadly, Joseph began to seek the company of unmarried women in his congregation. There is no evidence of physical impropriety, but a very bad example was set. He recognised how wrong this was, yet failed to take steps to avoid temptation:

> At the building a great deal including with Mr Marsden. Drank tea and spent the evening at Mr Rouse's. I always enjoy Miss Rouse's company. I wish I could keep away as it fills me with dislike to Mrs H, but I cannot help loving her. She was very free this evening in stating various things. She placed great confidence in me and I in her. O that neither of us may abuse it.

Ann was behaving very strangely at the same time:

> Last night Mrs H did as she has done several times lately, to my great distress. She jumped out of bed, ran into the garden in her night gown and made me go there from a warm bed to get her in. She then threatened to get out at

the window, all this time she seemed quite sensible and afterwards said she hated, despised and abhorred herself for her conduct to her husband and minister, and said there could be no hope for her soul. Hereupon I got myself to console her with the truths of the gospel but love her I cannot. Frequent improper conduct has taken away even that good which I wished of her and has revived in me these latest disaffections which I have frequently displayed.

Herrick's response to Ann's problems was inexcusable. It is evident that he was selfishly preoccupied with his own condition and blind to the reasons for his wife's unusual behaviour. We know from previous diary entries that he was expecting an addition to his family, yet we read the diary entry for later the same day:

NB this afternoon, about 3 o'clock, my wife was unexpectedly delivered of a son.

Herrick is clearly seen here as a flawed character, seeking the wrong company and unwilling to attend to his wife's needs. If we are honest, though, we recognise that depression is often very selfish and can cause serious harm to those who are closest to us. We shall see that Herrick was heading for a full-blown mental breakdown. This lack of love to his wife was something he was ashamed of—the phrase above from 'but love her I cannot' to 'disaffections I have frequently displayed,' is crossed out in the diary by a later pen of a different colour. We believe it was a temporary phase which did change for good when Herrick's and Ann's health changed for the better.

After the birth, trials did not slacken in their intensity for the next six weeks as the couple looked after their very sick and premature child. How tragic to report at the end:

Slept alone last night, awoke in the morning with the cries

of my wife who stood by my bedside, and in the utmost agony presented to me the breathless corpse of my child who died between 5 and 7 while she was asleep. Went for Mr Lester and the doctor, a great deal agitated. But I bless God he has taken from a world of sin and sorrow, to one of glory and happiness. May it be sanctified to us both for Christ's sake. Preached at Helens Lane morning and afternoon, well attended. Several friends called upon us …

The Lord brought them through this severe trial, and Herrick continued his ministry in the partly constructed new building — nothing would ever keep him from his God-given service, yet his nerves had been shattered by the tragedy, and permanent damage must have been done to his personality.

The birth of Ann Douglas and the temporary collapse of Herrick's health

Towards the end of June 1817 Herrick commenced a new outlet of Christian service: he began writing. He started in a small way with an essay: 'Man, as to his present state and future destiny.' The essay was described as a little book in March 1818, 500 copies being printed by his good friend Thomas Marsden. No copy of this book has been discovered, but only two months later he began a far more onerous task: that of answering his Unitarian critics with a Biblical demonstration of the truth about the person and work of Christ. The title of the book is long-winded: 'Immanuel, being a collection of scriptures relating to the person and work of the Lord Jesus Christ with cursory remarks in twenty-five letters to a friend designed to shew that the Bible is against Socinians.' We shall refer to it simply as 'Immanuel.'

Writing Immanuel was a very taxing proposition in 1818,

especially as his wife Ann was pregnant again. In August, he admitted as much in his diary.

In that same month, Herrick was hit very hard by a bout of depression. He recorded in his diary on Sunday August 23, 1818:

Preached at Helens Lane morning and afternoon. At home in the evening. Mr Thornton called and Mr and Mrs Nash. I was very low and nervous, and have been so ever since last Monday. Greatly distressed by the fear of death, which I pray God to sanctify to the promotion of holiness in heart and life.

As a true Christian, he committed himself to God in prayer, recording on three successive days:

O Lord. May I have to record a sanctified result of my very painful experience. O, raise me above the fear of dying, by faith in thy dear Son, Amen.

Preached at Helens Lane, but still exceedingly low in mind and body. O Lord, be merciful to me, and deliver me from these distressing apprehensions by an increase of grace. I beg it for Christ's sake. Lord, grant it, Amen.

Left off study for a few days. Took a long walk. Some medicine etc. Lord, bless the means I use, and raise me up and make me stronger in faith and more devoted to thee, for Christ's sake.

Why did Herrick suffer this severe depression? There seem to have been two main contributing causes. Reading between the lines, his wife's third pregnancy seems to have been the main catalyst. He clearly dreaded the possibility of a third death in the family; the nearer the due date approached, the more Herrick seems to have assumed that it was his own death that was imminent. The second contribution was surely the intense study involved in writing Immanuel. Many whole days were spent with hardly any social contact. The act of writing involved him delving to some extent into the soul-destroying doctrines of Unitarianism. This writer can attest to the depressing effect this can have, if great care is not taken: a little poison does the heart no good; as the Scriptures assure us: 1 Corinthians 5:6 … 'Do you not know that a little leaven leavens the whole lump?' The preaching continued unabated, but the passages he chose to cast into sermons increasingly reflected his own struggles: as Psalm 119:153, 'Consider my affliction and deliver me; for I do not forget thy law.' Friends invited him for meals and relaxation, but though the place changed, the pain remained. He would weep and pray, but find no relief. Fear of death was probably not unusual in one sense: Herrick lived in an age where mortality rates were high, especially among infants, but also among adults. Late October was Ann's due date; In early September Herrick actually missed a church meeting 'by reason of affliction.' By the end of September Joseph had reached crisis point, feeling so unwell that he left his diary untouched till the beginning of November. He decided to 'escape' from Colchester and stayed at various homes in the county until 29 October. On his return, he was delighted to discover that his wife had been safely delivered of 'a lovely little girl,' healthy and charming—she had arrived just the day before. It is surely no coincidence that the last record of the state of his health was only three days after his daughter's birth, indicating that he was 'still very fatigued, but not as bad as he had been.' The relief of discovering a healthy daughter and a happy wife at home was clearly the tonic he needed. He could come home for good, he recorded!

The Unitarians were also giving Herrick cause for concern in 1818. The Old Meeting room in Helens Lane was reroofed and the chapel opened as a Unitarian place of worship only 50 yards away! Herrick was worrying unnecessarily about this. Most Unitarian meetings in the land had only a few dozen in the congregation, and this was the case in Helens Lane too. During most of 1818 Herrick could not be certain of this outcome; in fact, he worried that there might be a thinning of his own congregation on the first evening, but this did not happen. This constant concern made the writing of Immanuel urgent and stressful.

All in all, 1818 was a year of sharp trial, but one of eventual victory through God's grace to his servant.

Chapter 9
Herrick's relationships with other ministers

Herrick's relationship with local congregational ministers was very much coloured by their response to his problems during the Unitarian crisis. Herrick expressed disappointment on a number of occasions because they would take no side in the dispute, and although expressing a degree of sympathy, did little to help him. At the point when Herrick was beginning to collect money for a new building in July 1816, he went to a few local ministers to ask for their support. Neither John Savill of the Colchester Lion Walk church nor William Hordle the minister in the Harwich church offered encouragement or would support his letter to beg for money.

The nub of the problem lay with the character of Independent churches. Independence meant exactly that—it was understood as 'non-interference:' let every church do what is right before the Lord. As churches and believers, they had suffered so much from the state church in previous centuries, a dogma of non-intervention was part of their DNA. James Bennett in his history of Dissenters agrees with this analysis:[115]

> A tendency to rivalry in the churches, instead of regarding the prosperity of each one as the gain of the whole, may, perhaps, be said to be the natural fruit of Independency.

Colchester's Independent ministers

John Savill (1780–1836), took his first ministerial role as morning preacher at Salters Hall in London, before being called to Lion Walk in 1809. The feeling between Herrick and Savill seems to have been particularly strong: their churches were less than 400 metres apart, in a town whose population was around 14,000 in 1821.[116] They were both able to sustain large congregations, up to 1000 strong, but for the first time, from 1814 onwards, there was competition between two Independent churches in the town, and the relationship between them was not always comfortable.

The main cause of friction was the hurt caused by members of one church wishing to switch allegiance to the other. This was rightly deemed a breaking of the covenant made between members on a regular basis. It denied the reality of local church fellowship. It did not agree with the Bible view of believers within it depicted as joined together as members of the same body, rejoicing with those who rejoiced, suffering alongside those who suffered. The drift of church members was largely from Lion Walk to Stockwell chapel, and it started as early as 1817. One can sympathise with Savill on receiving the curt letters below from Messrs Simpson and Blomfield, with not a word of thanks or recognition of the broken bond:

Revd Sir,

I have been in the habit for some time past of attending the Ministry of Mr Herrick and as it is my desire to continue my attendance, I have to request of you, and the Church over which you are Pastor, to favour me with my Dismission from thence, as early as convenient.

I am Sir

Yours most obediently,

Henry Simpson

22 Culver Street   26th February 1817

Dear Sir,

Having heard Mr Herrick I hope with Profit, I think of continuing to attend on his ministry and as I intend to Communicate with the People of his Charge I would thank you for my Dismission from your church,

I remain with the greatest respect

Dear Sir, your Sincere Friend,

Samuel Blomfield

John Savill's reply to these two men gave full vent to the feelings of betrayal felt by members, pastor and deacons at Lion Walk.[117]

Savill letter to Henry Simpson and Samuel Blomfield on their request for dismission from Lion Walk

Christian Friend

You having applied for your dismission from our Communion we have agreed to send you the same, but lament that we should have reason to complain of the circumstances under which the application is made. It appears to us truly deplorable that any professors of religion of our denomination should be so unacquainted with, or indifferent to, the obligations which devolve upon each individual member of a Christian Church, as to dissolve the bonds of union without even a reference to their existence. The irregularity of your conduct in communicating with another church in the Town, while that to which you voluntarily joined yourself was assembled at the sacred Table—that too without intimating your intention either to your Pastor or your Brethren—your withdrawing yourself from them without stating a single objection to their doctrine, conduct or discipline, or so much as expressing the least sentiment of regard for them as a Church, or regret that any circumstances should have led to a separation, discovers, in our view, a turn of mind so capricious, and in its tendency so subversive of the principles and order upon which the apostolic Churches were built and by which their conduct was regulated, as at once to excite our surprise and lamentation. As you have not solicited any commendation to any other Church, it would be improper in us to offer one.

Sincerely wishing you however a large increase of spiritual benefit from this ministry you may hereafter attend, with real prosperity of soul, and a maturity for joining the glorious assembly of the Church of the Firstborn in Heaven, we as a Christian Society do, at your request dismiss you from our fellowship.

Signed in behalf of the Church,

(Pastor and Deacons)

A copy of the above is transmitted to Mr S— he having applied for his Dismission under the same circumstances.

The sentiments expressed here are truly Biblical, but it is a pity they were not expressed privately to Herrick. The church members involved may well have been embarrassed about the situation and ignorant of church etiquette. It is likely that they were anxious about breaking the news to Savill, and not very competent letter writers. Feathers were unnecessarily ruffled, and Herrick was increasingly regarded by the Lion's Walk deacons as a trouble maker. It was not Herrick's fault that his preaching may well have been more attractive than Savill's, and so more likely to bring people to hear him.

Matters got even worse when Joseph and Elizabeth Bugg requested dismission to Stockwell Chapel in two polite letters written to the Lion Walk church in November 1822. By August of 1823, no communication had been received from pastor Savill, so Herrick sent the following letter:

Aug 8, 1823

Dear Sir,

Joseph Bugg and his wife were proposed as candidates for communion with our church last Friday.

We have kept them waiting so long that we feel it our duty to come to some decision and shall therefore be glad to receive some *official* information from you concerning them—particularly whether their relation with you is *entirely dissolved* and if so on what grounds?

We should also be happy to know why those who communed with you are judged unfit to be dismissed to a neighbouring church? And why some of your Members say they might have been dismissed to any other Independent church than ours?

Information on these points would greatly assist our Members at their next Ch meeting and, particularly

Yours very respectfully,

Joseph Herrick

Nine months was far too long a delay, but again, why did they not have a private conversation rather than write a letter which 200 years later is there for all to see in the Church Minute Book? Savill had good reason not to dismiss the couple: he said dismission to another church implied recommendation. He felt very happy to recommend Elizabeth Bugg, but quite unable to do the same for her husband. They were left with a quandary; how could they justify a split decision? Lion Walk would dismiss them 'into the world' as it were, and let the Stockwell church decide about church membership, knowing the full details.

Then Savill adds this coda:

Sir, no doubt it affords you infinite satisfaction, the having accomplished the darling object of your mind, that of adding afflictions to affliction. May it bring you all pleasure your soul can bear. I beseech you to read the 12 v of ch 3 of the epistle to James and the 3 v of the 7 chapter of Matthew and no doubt you will remember Nathan's reply to David, go on to triumph and remember you too must give account. Eli spoke harshly to Hannah and he died with a broken neck.

This comment is remarkably savage, and surely unmerited. Savill completely changed his mind about Herrick not many years later. After resigning from Lion Walk in 1828 and a disastrous two-year pastorship nearby in Halstead, he sat under Herrick's ministry for the last few years of his life until his death in 1836. It is touching to read Herrick's final comment:[118]

Mr John Savill very ill, the Minister with him so as not to be at Church till ½ past 7. We fear we shall lose him who has been a communicant a long time and a great help in our late expensive alterations, his mind peacefully relies on the truth of God in the gospel.

This entry shows the two men united in true Christian fellowship in the end, a testimony to the healing power of the gospel and Biblical forgiveness.

Henry March (1791–1869) was first called to minister at Bungay Congregational church, Suffolk; then he became chaplain at Mill Hill school before being called to Lion Walk shortly after Savill's resignation. Relations between Herrick and March seem to have been much more fraught than between Herrick and Savill, and it is not totally clear why this was so. As with Savill, the main contributing factor seems to have been the way in which people moved between the two churches. Herrick seems to have been a stickler for correct procedure, and he was clearly upset when one lady member moved from Stockwell Chapel to Lion Walk and was allowed to benefit from membership there without any reference to the previous church she had been to.[119]

The Stockwell Church Minute book is largely silent about the friction between the two Congregational churches in Colchester; reports in the newspapers give more information on this crucial matter. During the early 1830s March's church seems to have had a healthy increase in membership, but at the same time there was clearly a substantial drift of his congregation to Stockwell Chapel. This was one of the reasons for the large extension of Herrick's Chapel in 1836, though there is no hint of this in Stockwell's Minute book. An examination of this document reveals only five new members joining from Lion Walk at this time, and only one going in the opposite direction. Most of those who moved to Stockwell chapel must then have been only subscribers or hearers in the congregation. This is the only way we can match the data in the minute books with the insistence of Essex church historians and writers in the local papers at the time:[120, 121]

Subsequently the chapel underwent a second enlargement in order to accommodate a more numerous section of Dissenters who had seceded from the Lion Walk Chapel.

... there had for some time been 'painful hindrances' to his ministry (March's Ed.), including disputes which led to the departure of some of the congregation to St. Helen's Lane circa 1836.

Given the amount of aggravation Herrick experienced when he had to enlarge Stockwell Chapel, it would not surprise us if he blamed March for the problems, and considered the Lion Walk church to have been out of control.

Matters came to a head in 1839. This was the most disgraceful episode in Herrick's life, and little can be said to excuse what he said and did. The spark that lit the flame, was quite trivial. It was the custom, early in the new year, for the two Congregational ministers to take it in turns to preach at the Colchester alms houses. It was then the rule for the preacher's health to be drunk at a subsequent dinner. March preached that year, and Herrick refused to join in the toast. One of March's scheming deacons, Dr David Morris, noticed and stirred things up; March reacted by sending a mild letter of complaint, which was published in the local newspaper. Herrick, an irritable man by nature, rose to the bait, and gave back far more than it was worth—an outrageous letter, widely published, to the delight of the established church readership and to the dishonour of the gospel and the Lord's name. The letter exchange, as published in the local papers, is shown below.[122]

FROM MR. MARCH TO MR. HERRICK.

Dear Sir. The copy of your letter to Mr Morris received this morning, greatly surprised me, as I never had a word of conversation on the subject of it either with him or Mr J Darnell. (A copy of this letter to David Morris has not been found, Ed.) It is true, that having gone to the Gift House to hear you last year, I had hoped that my doing so might have been a beginning of more friendly intercourse between us and that if you returned my overture towards this, there would be, at least once a year, an opportunity of exchanging tokens of Christian kindness, which would be pleasant to ourselves and honourable to the blessed religion which we teach. Your declining this, and your afterwards refusing to notice me while you were yet sitting at the table when my health was drank, did certainly grieve me by disappointing the hope I had entertained. The only person to whom I have mentioned this (with the exception of one friend) are three of the deacons of my church, when together, to whom I expressed my regret, that my overture had failed, and that my hope had been disappointed: but I remember expressly saying, that I did not intend to take the matter up as an affront. I thought it best to say thus much by way of explanation, and now heartily commending you to the mercy and grace of our common Lord, I am, sincerely, your well-wisher,

(Signed)—HENRY MARCH.

MR. HERRICK'S ANSWER.

Messrs. March and Morris,

Gentlemen, I am sorry to learn, by a note received yesterday, who is really the author of this mean and unmanly attempt to injure me. I had hoped that D Morris had gone further than he ought to have done. I will not allow myself to say all I think of a minister who can entertain three of his deacons with a serious lamentation over such worldly nonsense. The animus of the whole thing is very clear, and the history of it would make good sport for the Philistines, especially if they were to draw the principal characters, as I feel that I most easily could. The one most soft and solemn, and to all appearance I trust really pious— very! as Fanny Kemble used to say; but fond of scandal in spite of his religion, more so than any woman I ever knew; and from him over his tea I have heard more than I ever did from any woman in my life in the same space of time; spiteful as a woman when excited, gossiping as a woman; obstinate as a woman; opinionated as a blue-stocking woman; and full of little resources as a woman against a rival. He ought to have been Henrietta; but men being sadly wanted, owing to the war became dear little Henry. The other more manly, daring, violent, malicious, not nice about times and terms, when carried away by his temper, or thinking his own interest will be promoted or another's impaired by anything he can do—fond of distinction, he is a valuable help to the former, and does what he would shrink from: and I have seen and heard so much of him, that I have seriously thought an octavo sheet would be well employed to set myself right with the people—or would an advertisement do best? Really, people ought to be guarded against him as against a wild animal that has got loose."

With good wishes, yours truly,

JOSEPH HERRICK.

The effect this letter had on Henry March was devastating to the church at Lion Walk. He felt quite unable to continue as a minister in Colchester, if there was a danger of such an attack again. His words in the Lion Walk church minute book are very telling:[123]

My dear Christian friends,

For a considerable time at intervals my mind has been a good deal discouraged by painful hindrances to my usefulness and comfort in this place … but latterly, my path has seemed to be increasingly difficult; and at length, an occurrence* has taken place so shocking to my spirit, and presenting, in my apprehension, so great an obstacle to the progress of good, as to have led me to a serious review of my position here. The result is, a conviction that my continuance in this post would be attended with imminent hazard to my health; and that there is little hope of any greatly beneficial change, but by the blessing of God on a new ministry in this place ...

*(Deacon's added note)—This alludes to a scurrilous and infamous letter, quite unprovoked, sent to the pastor by Joseph Herrick, Independent Minister in this town, whose own people, stung with shame, sent him a remonstrance, and at length wrung from him a note of apology ...

The same paper describes the stinging response Herrick got from the women in his own church:

The ladies rose up as one woman to resist the indignity offered to the female character. Obstinate as a woman! fond of scandal as a woman! spiteful as a woman! were expressions in everybody's mouth. It was at one time feared there would have been a petticoat rebellion; and at the very least, that Mr. Herrick would have had his ears pulled. But the sex are forgiving: a remonstrance having been sent to the offender by his leading hearers, and he having apologized for the personal offence; and having, 'in his place,' made the *amende honorable* to the outraged virtues of the ladies, by telling them that women were much better than men; and moreover, possessing (a very strong point that!) the title deeds of his own chapel, the affair has been allowed to blow over.

The only thing that could be said in defence of this sorry incident, is that the letter was *not* entirely unprovoked. David Morris's evil eye encouraged the plot: he had ulterior motives in fomenting opposition at Stockwell Chapel. It seems that this event catalysed a long season of trouble for Herrick, lasting from early 1839 until its resolution more than four years later. This will be fully discussed in Chapter 10. His experience in those difficult years should be viewed as God's chastisement of his wayward child, purifying major flaws in his character.

The Bible is clear that though confessed sin in a believer can be forgiven, nevertheless, our Father in heaven allows us to undergo Fatherly discipline, to teach us His truth, and correct our failings. Hebrews 12:6 tells us: 'for whom the Lord loves he chastens, and scourges every son whom he receives.'

March was succeeded at Lion Walk by Thomas Davids (1816–1884), who was called to the pastorate in 1841. Herrick's relationship with Davids was much more convivial than that with March. They were similarly fiery in nature. Herrick also saw in Davids' problems at the start of his pastorate, parallels with his own at Helens Lane. This must have drawn his sympathy. Since he had caused so much difficulty during March's pastorate, he must have been much more cautious in his dealings with his successor. Davids was an out and out evangelist like Herrick, having much success in creating new preaching stations outside Colchester, and with his first wife Louisa seeing a massive increase in Sunday School blessing. In the 12 years before her early death, the numbers rose from 200 to 750, with teacher involvement enlarged from 20 to 70.[124] By 1845, no less than 33 scholars had been received into church fellowship.[125] Herrick joined with Davids in supporting a number of evangelistic causes. One particular shared interest was the Colchester Town Mission,[126] whose aim was 'to reclaim the drunkard, the sabbath breaker, the profane swearer, and the unfortunate degraded female.' The labourers in this mission had visited 1,730 of the 1,743 families in Colchester during 1846. The success of the mission was summarised as:

joined Christian churches	4
died in hope	6
cases of hopeful change	4
drunkards reclaimed	2
fallen females reclaimed	4

the ruin of one youthful female ... prevented	1
induced to attend public worship	10

What an amazing level of activity this short summary encompasses, and what a gospel blessing! In 1844, Herrick and Davids joined many other ministers in prayer and practical support of Christians who were in hardship in Scotland following the disruption of the Church of Scotland, and the creation of the Free Church of Scotland.[127] Both men spoke at the meeting, and large collections were sent to help their Scottish brethren in their hour of need. Herrick and Davids were still cooperating as late as 1862 at a meeting[128]

> to consider the propriety of petitioning the Legislature for the prevention of the sale of intoxicating liquors on the Sabbath day.

London ministers

Outside Colchester, Herrick enjoyed warm fellowship with a good number of ministers, by no means all of them from an Independent background. One notable preacher he came to know in London, just after his conversion was John Hyatt (1767–1826). Herrick became a pupil of Hyatt, and ever after was on very friendly terms with him. He got him to speak to his people as early as 1816 and had the privilege of preaching at Tottenham Court Chapel and the Tabernacle in July 1818. Hyatt was very much in the line of George Whitefield, being converted under one of his successors at the Tabernacle. It was said of Hyatt that none of Whitefield's successors was better adapted than he to follow in his steps. Before he came to London he was a gifted and successful field preacher in Sherborne. His preaching was noted for its ability to delineate the human character to the discomfort of his hearers. His appeals to the conscience were like thunder to some, and although his aim was always to be experimental, he was most winsome in his soul-searching preaching. Herrick could not have had a better role model, and his frequent visits to London tell us how valued his preaching became in the line of Calvinistic Methodists. Of his other London friends, we need to add to what we have said about Thomas Wilson (1774–1843). Although not a minister, Wilson was highly influential on a spiritual level to many of the students at Hoxton academy and later Highbury College. As we have seen, Wilson's parents were saved under Whitefield's preaching in London, and the son had very much the same evangelical Calvinistic convictions. He showed a fatherly interest in the students, wishing most of all to know how they were getting on with their preaching. One student noted the kind and affectionate remarks he made:[129]

> He would say with the characteristic rubbing of his hands: 'Never forget the three Rs—Ruin, Redemption, and Regeneration. Keep to these and you will never fail. They will always supply you with plenty of matter for the whole course of your ministry.'

Wilson was a wealthy man, his inheritance coming from his parent's work in the burgeoning silk trade. He used his money most generously. He supported the construction of new Independent chapels all around the country, as well as helping struggling causes, such as Helens Lane in Colchester at the beginning. Herrick never lost his admiration and love for this man, and his debt was spiritual as well as material.

Ministers from the Established Church and the Methodists

Some may be surprised to learn that although Herrick was a Dissenter, he was happy to listen to gospel men from the

Established Church. Good came from one such visit in 1844, as a recently widowed member of Stockwell Chapel recalled.[130] He met Herrick one evening, some days after Herrick had advised him to remarry, if he met a suitable lady.

> I was at St. Peter's Church one Thursday evening, as was the custom of Mr Herrick himself sometimes, to hear Mr Carr. After leaving the Church … I passed a young woman by the name of Esther Groves, whom I had seen before, but never to know her … I found she knew my deceased wife and had heard of me … I courted her some weeks … We were married by Joseph Herrick, August 14, 1844.

Finally, we should note that Herrick had fellowship with Wesleyan Methodists through much of his ministerial career, even though one could have understood if his Calvinistic beliefs cautioned against it. As many as 16 people from a Methodist background became members at Stockwell. Herrick preached occasionally at Methodist chapels in the Colchester area, and in the last 30 years he had a close friendship with William Steadman, a Methodist missionary. It was this man who spoke to his grieving congregation on the Sunday after Herrick's death: a surprising turn of events yet showing the breadth of his Christian heart.

Chapter 10
The 4-year plot to eject Herrick from Stockwell Chapel: 1839–1843[131]

The trouble between Herrick and March in January 1839 turned out to be the opening shots of what became an all-out war conducted by some who wanted Herrick out of Stockwell Chapel. The issue between March and Herrick was a smokescreen, to divert attention from the true protagonists and to hide their plans. To provide a background we need to consider two things: firstly, the prevailing attitude of some Dissenters in Colchester, and secondly the main architect behind the plan.

Colchester's Dissenters after the Reform Act of 1832

The Reform Act of 1832 sought to put right the political misrepresentation of the people in parliament, eliminating the 'rotten boroughs' where a few wealthy patrons had more representation than large modern cities. This was especially interesting to some Dissenters who had also been restricted in their careers and involvement in public life by the 17th century Test and Corporation Acts of parliament. Only men who partook of the Lord's Supper according to the rite of the Church of England had been allowed these privileges of public engagement. Dissenters had been counted out. Also, they had been denied high-flying careers in the military or legal profession or political life, and never enjoyed an Oxford or Cambridge education. When these two acts were repealed in 1828, all these things changed for Dissenters.

The two Congregational churches in Colchester took opposite

views on whether their members should now seek involvement in political life, particularly. Herrick always made sure he was well informed about political developments and would make representation to the authorities if the moral or spiritual welfare of his congregation were threatened. He joined, for example, in appealing against the imposition of the Church Rate, which unfairly demanded that Dissenters contribute towards the maintenance of the State Church. We have seen, also, that he appealed against the sale of alcoholic beverages on the Lord's Day. When it came to active involvement in public political life, however, Herrick never encouraged it. He felt this was a distraction from the gospel work of the church. Also, many of the members at Stockwell Chapel were poor people who could never be involved with politics and public life; statements about political involvement would only be divisive. Lion Walk church, on the other hand, had significantly more members from the moneyed class; this is evident from the number of esquires in the church. John Savill was well to do; his parents were involved in the silk trade, and he was distantly related by marriage to the Wilsons from London—the same family as Herrick's mentor, Thomas Wilson. Savill's sons George, Robert Maitland and Joseph were all wealthy and influential men. Phillips tells us that:[132]

Lion Walk Congregational Church supplied 19 Liberal mayors and 61 Liberal town councillors in 100 years.

Thus, we can see different views prevailed among Independents in Colchester in the 1830s.

Even more ambitious Dissenters in Colchester

The level of social and political involvement among members at Lion Walk was still not enough for some of them. Chief among these was a medical doctor, David Morris, whom we have already met in the March—Herrick letter exchange. He had joined Lion Walk from Dundee in September 1823. His organisational abilities led quite soon to his involvement as a deacon under John Savill. Morris pushed for change during much of the time he was at Lion Walk; discontent spread to other church members, including John Chaplin a fellow deacon. Matters came to a climax in 1828 when three resignation letters reached John Savill within two days. The pastor noted in the church minute book:[133]

> … John Chaplin had called upon me on Wednesday last and signified his determination of withdrawing from the Church and that he should commune with us no more, in consequence of the unsettled state of his mind. On the same day I received the attached note from James Carter signifying the same determination which I then read, and next I read a similar note from David Morris, which had been put into my hand a few minutes before …

Morris's letter is enigmatic, indicating unrest in the church, but giving no reasons:[134]

> To Revd John Savill
>
> Reverend Sir,
>
> From a number of causes I have felt very uncomfortable in connexion with the Church over which you preside—and that too at various points over the last <u>two</u> years.
>
> To detail these causes would lead to us good practical result. My conversation with you at your house some months ago will supply some of them—the others may as well for the sake of peace be buried in oblivion.
>
> After having weighed the whole matter deliberately, and asked I trust, Divine direction; I have thought it best to

dissolve my relation with the church, and do accordingly beg to be considered as no longer a member thereof.

With many thanks for past kindness (which I assure you I wish duly to appreciate) and sincere prayers for your prosperity both in public and private,

I am,

> Reverend Sir
>
> Your faithful servant,
>
> David Morris

Head Street

30 May, 1828

The coincidence of three significant members wishing to leave at once, has the look of a careful Morris' plan to maximise the stress to the minister: it certainly had that effect. Savill wrote a resignation letter shortly afterwards.

Henry March was appointed as pastor, first on the recommendation of John Savill, and later of the church. He commenced officially on November 18, 1829. We then find Morris back in the Lion Walk membership as early as February 5, 1830, less than three months after March's induction service! The minute book calmly observes:[135]

> February 5, 1830. Mr Morris having signified his wish to return to the communion of the church, it was agreed that he should be re-admitted.

What was happening over the next nine years before the infamous Herrick-March exchange of letters? We know there was a steady trickle of Lion Walk's congregation who became listeners at Stockwell Chapel. Three of these were trustees of

Lion Walk, two of whom were solicitors. One gets the distinct impression that members of the two Independent congregations lived in each other's pockets; much of what was going on in one church was shared with the other. This could work in a good way, as when John Savill, with George and Maitland his sons, contributed generously to the new extension of Stockwell Chapel.[136] It worked quite the other way when trustees and solicitors, originally from Lion Walk, interfered with the management of Stockwell. One writer has even suggested that this was all part of a plot managed by Morris, who encouraged the migration to Stockwell in order to set up a fifth column[137] in a chapel he wished to take over![138] This is difficult to prove, but we do know that at the time when March and Herrick fell out, the tactics used by the Lion Walk deacons were particularly distasteful. An anonymous member of March's congregation wrote to J.B. Harvey, editor of the Mercury, on 22nd March 1839, saying that:[139]

> the conduct of some of his (i.e. March's) Church, Messrs. Morris, F. Bridge and others has throughout the whole affair been most disgraceful and shows that they think no method bad enough to prop up the cause of their own Chapel at the expense of that of the other.

Reading between the lines, it was probably at this point that Morris began to think seriously about planning for a third Congregational church in Colchester. Maybe Phillips is correct.[140] Perhaps Morris was thinking along the lines: if Herrick is vulnerable, maybe he can be forced out of his chapel, and I and my supporters can take over the church and convert it into the sort of church we want. Morris's thoughts about a third church were kept strictly secret; but they were widely publicised immediately after the attempt to oust Herrick failed (see information later). The small print, following NB, in the flyer below, published in June 1843, is interesting.

Divine Worship.

attendance morning 200 evening 350

THE

LARGE ROOM, LION WALK,

COLCHESTER,

HAVING BEEN ENGAGED FOR PUBLIC WORSHIP,

THE OPENING SERVICES

WILL TAKE PLACE

On SUNDAY, JUNE the 25th, 1843,

WHEN TWO

SERMONS

WILL BE PREACHED BY THE

REV. E. MIALL,

OF LONDON.

Service in the Morning to commence at a Quarter before Eleven, and in the Evening at Half-past Six.

N. B.—These services have been commenced by Christian Friends, who, in common with others, have long felt the importance of extending the cause of Religion in Colchester, by means of an additional Congregational Church, which in due time they hope, under the Divine Blessing, to see established.— The attendance and co-operation of such as are favorable to the object, are respectfully invited.

NO COLLECTION.

HARVEY, PRINTER, 95, HIGH STREET, COLCHESTER.

Figure 10: Flyer for first meeting of third Congregational church in June, 1843[141]

The need for this third church had long been felt, according to this flyer. What would be its unique characteristics? This was widely publicised in 1846, when Morris joined with the Colchester publisher J.B. Harvey, in a projected Newspaper, to be called the *Essex News and Colchester and East Anglian*

Advertiser. The views expressed would be:[142]

> consonant with the views of the advocates of Civil, Religious, and Commercial Freedom, who constitute a large and influential portion of the county of Essex.

Phillips has an intriguing picture of the members of this eventual third Congregational church on Sunday afternoon. The caption reads:[143]

> Earnest Nonconformists attend the Pleasant Sunday Afternoon at Headgate Chapel where burning moral issues of the day were expounded to receptive audiences.

This socially active agenda was desired by Morris and other Dissenters in Colchester: for those in the middle and upper strata of society. Morris realised this could rarely be provided at Lion Walk, and never at Stockwell Chapel.

Trouble breaks out at Stockwell chapel

It cannot be a coincidence that, within a month of the infamous letter exchange, a battle broke out at Stockwell Chapel. The main cause of the conflict lay with the enlargement of the chapel three years before. The outstanding debt for this extension was £300–£400. People began to demand answers to questions like: who is paying the interest on the debt? Who are the creditors? What about the trust deeds of the new chapel, and who are its trustees? Ought not the finances to be under the control of church deacons?

Questions relating to deeds had been raised before the building work had begun, by one of Herrick's congregation, Samuel Wittey, a solicitor. Wittey also happened to be one of the trustees of the Lion Walk church. His letter to Herrick has been preserved among family memorabilia:[144]

My dear Sir,

I have satisfied myself beyond the possibility of doubt, that the writings of Mr Bridge's home do not comprise the Title to the Meeting House. As I conjectured the Mill House which formerly stood there and Mr Sudell's house, at one time belonged to the same person and Mr Keep of whom Jackson purchased, derived the Mill house from a source quite different to that thru which he took the dwelling house ...

You will I think agree with me that it is the duty of the trustees to find up and possess themselves of the Title Deeds of the present building before more money is expended upon it, and that you may search amongst such documents as you possess and make enquiries amongst the parties concerned when the Mill house was bought, is the object of my troubling you with this and hoping that you may be able to acquire some information on the subject before I see you in the evening,

I remain my dear Sir,

yours sincerely

Samuel Wittey

Whether Herrick did as Wittey suggested, we have no way of finding out. But the issue of the trust deeds was a subject mentioned frequently in Stockwell church meetings especially from 1839 onwards.

The deacon trouble at Stockwell chapel

Within a month of the rift between March and Herrick the men at Stockwell chapel asked for something which had never been done there before: a special church meeting to which only men members would be invited. Ostensibly, the meeting was requested to choose a set of new deacons. In fact, the church already had a group of deacons: there was no urgent need for more. In truth, Herrick had had nothing but trouble from some of his deacons, from the very beginning. When Philip Hunt resigned from the diaconate for not working with the other deacons, and having Hypercalvinist views, Herrick wrote in the minute book:[145]

> ... no other person will be appointed to the office you have vacated, unless Providence should send us somebody remarkably suitable, as I have been peculiarly unfortunate in the article of Deacons ...

The chief target for the new deacons was, undoubtedly, the second resolution made that night:[146]

> That the deacons shall have the entire management of the temporal concerns of the church—and of the Church funds.

They wanted to control the finances, especially the church debt. This only became clear very much later. The proximity of this sudden outburst of trouble to the differences with the Lion Walk church is very striking. The ruse of 'men only' voting had been used by the Lion Walk church after Savill's resignation 10 years earlier.[147] This would only have been known by Lion Walk church members, who, we presume, passed this information on to the Stockwell church people.

Months and months of wrangling followed, before a group of four deacons finally agreed to serve and promised to work with the pastor. Sadly, even though a binding agreement was signed by the pastor and deacons, Herrick had to report in January 1840:[148]

> The last year has been one of the most painful and trying this Church ever passed through. Everything has been done

by several with a view to injure the Minister in his credit, acceptance, usefulness and comfort. Prayer meetings have been neglected by many, and most of all by those whose duty it was to have attended them. The amount of untruth has been very terrible. Men of long standing as professors have been betrayed into the most direct and unquestionable falsehoods, and the solemn agreement written and signed on Aug 2, 1839 … has not been regarded, the parties up to this time not having consulted each other any more than before … *private meetings* all through the year have been frequent, to *only one* of which was the Minister invited. Lord, what is man!

The solicitors create more trouble at Stockwell chapel

In January 1840, Herrick's opponents took a new line of attack. Samuel Wittey the lawyer joined hands with another solicitor John Stuck Barnes and tried to force Herrick to resign his place on the Trust deeds of Stockwell chapel. The choice of Barnes was very clever: he was the son-in-law of James Nash, Herrick's senior deacon, who had been his chief friend for more than 25 years. Would divided loyalty get Nash on their side? The lawyers' argument was that the original trust deed for the chapel built in 1816 needed updating. They had, without Herrick's consent, chosen new trustees for the new deed, and wanted him to sign a new document handing over control to them. Their real motive in all this was obvious to Herrick:[149]

(they) want to get me out of the trust that they may mortgage the chapel and have the control of its funds.

Because Herrick did not trust them, he steadfastly refused to bow to their will, even though Maitland Savill, now one of his enemies, threatened he would never give another farthing of his money to the cause at Stockwell chapel, if he did not. At the end of a very long meeting, Herrick offered to sign their documents provided:[150]

> they would sign *a declaration* guaranteeing me against interruption ... and pledging themselves not to mortgage the chapel. But they refused to do so.

Everything changed five days later when Herrick finally agreed to sign their deed. He was utterly weary of all the strife and felt that a promise from Nash that the chapel would *not* be mortgaged could be trusted. He also had a strong desire to end a contest which many of the members did not understand. This had led to a breakdown of relationships between those in the know and those who were mystified by the whole event.[151]

We probably need to explain the use of the term 'mortgage,' in the current context. There was an outstanding debt following the enlargement of the chapel. We do not know to whom this money was owed, but clearly debt repayments at some rate of interest were required: this was called a mortgage. Wittey and Barnes had clearly taken over the management of this debt and were using it as a bargaining chip with the deacons to force Herrick out of the church.

Broken promises lead to broken friendships

It was not long before Nash's promise, that the chapel would not be mortgaged, was shown to be utterly hollow. Nash was in an impossible position, between the immovable rock of his pastor's will to stay on for the sake of his flock, and the hard place of his son-in-law's determination to eject a domineering minister by manipulating the chapel debt. Nash, unfortunately, sided with John Barnes, and joined his fellow deacons, Hunt,

Hubbard and Lester, in doing all they could to weaken Herrick's position. Hard things were said, both at regular church meetings and in special meetings convened by the deacons and debt controllers. This was followed by the disastrous actions of an anonymous letter writer who took advantage of the disorderly state of the church to send a missive to many church members with wild accusations against two of Herrick's opponents. There was now so little respect between Herrick and his opponents that, with plenty of evidence to the contrary, Herrick's wife Ann was accused of being the author!

The upshot of all the aggression and disagreement was that all the deacons and many of their supporters left the church during the summer of 1840. The loss of such friends as George Lester and James Nash, who had stood with Herrick during the Unitarian crisis, must have been a hard blow to take. This did not happen, until the deacons and the lawyers had made one final effort to gain control of the chapel. A meeting was called in late April 1840, supposedly to discuss paying off the debt. This was deceitful, because the lawyers were adamant that they did not want the debt to be paid off. This is evident by the response to John Green at this meeting:[152]

> Mr John Green nobly offered to settle all dispute about the money by taking the whole debt upon himself and to pay it in four years, but though the sufficiency of his property was admitted, his offer was utterly refused!

This final meeting was 'useful' in a historical sense, in showing exactly who was ranged against Herrick. Five of the Lion Walk' trustees were now controlling the event: J.S. Barnes, W. Griffin, T. Moore, S. Wittey, and George Savill. The last of these now had two of his brothers present: R. Maitland Savill who had been a member since October 1832, but had joined those who objected to Herrick's ministry, and for the first time, his brother

Joseph, also a member of the opposition. George Savill took it upon himself to chair the meeting, not at the pastor and church member's request, but that of the lawyers.

In all these severe afflictions, Herrick was able to take a Christian view of their purpose:[153]

It is now however apparent to many who could not see it before, that the drift of all that has been doing for so long a time is to drive me from a station which I have occupied with considerable usefulness though with great unworthiness for nearly 27 years ... I have no right to complain of Providence and will not. The cup which is given me, shall I not drink it? Lord, help me to do it without a murmur, and be merciful to us yet, for His sake whose cause it is, and not mine, for which I am anxious!

Temporary peace reigns

Because of the disorder in the early part of 1840, church meetings had been cancelled at Stockwell chapel. Mercifully, the trouble had died down by September, so Herrick was able to record in the minute book:[154]

The Church, which has been kept in a very unhappy state by for a long time by Chisholm, Holland, Hunt, Nash, Hubbard and Lester, is now apparently getting more tranquil. Many malcontents have left. Happy had it been for the church and for their own souls, had they left much sooner. All was peaceful this evening.

This peaceful state of affairs lasted through the whole of 1841, and into the early months of 1842. This was a time of great blessing on the word preached. In the three years 1841 to 1843 more than 80 people were added to the church: new converts, as well as restored backsliders. In April 1841, the minister was happy to write of the pious feelings which showed itself in church meetings once more.[155]

In December 1841, Herrick wrote of the clear proof that the Lord's work was progressing in the church again.[156]

Unbeknown to the believers at Stockwell, however, trouble was bubbling below the surface, and in April of 1842 a notice of ejectment was served on Herrick and the pew opener. The instigators of this new development were the two lawyers Wittey and Barnes, with the support of W. Griffin—all three of them Lion Walk Trustees. Herrick commented:[157]

> The Cause prospers amidst all, God blessing his ordinances, man fighting against our peace. Some persons must have much to answer for.

Something very significant was happening about this time in Lion Walk church. David Morris was clearly not getting on with the new minister, Thomas Davids. Members of that church, and Davids had requested Morris to make up his mind, and on September 14, 1842, both he and his wife, in the convoluted language of the day, 'requested to be considered no longer members of your society.' David Morris expanded on the reason for this request, saying:

> ... after prayerful deliberation I believed it to be a duty imposed upon me, not from any change of sentiment either about Christian doctrines or Church order but from circumstances in *your* history as a church, which rendered my position such as prevented me from realizing any longer among *you* the great purposes of Christian fellowship, namely 'to *do* good, and to *get* good.

It was probably knowledge of this step on Morris's part that led Herrick to infer less than a week later that all was peace among them.[158]

The final stage of the attempt to oust Herrick

Herrick had rather misinterpreted Morris's plans after leaving Lion Walk! Morris, rather than being at peace, was now more desperate than ever to find a church home for socially and politically active Christians like himself. The time from September 1842 to February 1843 seems to have been used in organising the lawyers, Wittey and Barnes, rewriting the trust deed, obtaining those who could take over the Stockwell debt from the creditors and turning it into a 'mortgage' of the church. There is some uncertainty as to who the mortgagees actually were: Herrick mentions Barnes and Joseph Savill, whereas the Chelmsford Chronicle refers to Mr G. Lay, another of the Lion Walk deacons who had also been made a fictitious 'trustee' of Stockwell Chapel.

The enemies of Stockwell Chapel struck on Sunday, February 19, 1843. The description in the church minute book is vivid:[159]

An awful scene. The chapel seized by Sheriff's officers for a debt, nominally £714, due to Joseph Savill and John Stuck Barnes, 2 lawyers, to whom a pretended mortgage has been made by the trustees, in order to force the people to raise the money which they most unfairly claim. Under £300 is what appears to be really due on the chapel. The people were mixed with a multitude of people, many of them of the lowest description, getting their books, hassocks, cushions, flaps etc. which would otherwise have been put in the street. There was no need for this whatever as 4 distinct and anxious offers had been made to settle this matter, but nothing would satisfy the bitterness of some but this extreme measure, which will never be forgotten, and hardly forgiven, the indignation being so great in very many and the sorrow in distress in others.

If the debt had been £300 in 1836, it would have needed an exorbitant 12.5% compound interest rate to have grown to £714 in seven years. How terribly unjust of professing Christians to demand such a repayment but refuse to allow the debt to be settled! No wonder Herrick called the whole affair fictitious.

Twice in the space of 27 years Joseph Herrick had been forced out of his church building and prevented from preaching. Was ever a minister treated so badly? What made the issue even more distressing was the reports in the local press of this action and all the events that led up to it: all written by gloating Anglican sympathisers. How the Lord's name was brought into dishonour, and Dissenters in general shown to be nothing but unloving, unchristian troublemakers.

The settling of the debt and the return

Herrick *did* have an honest solicitor he could rely on. Mr W.W. Francis had been his chosen financial advisor when he first preached at Helens Lane in 1814, and throughout the Unitarian crisis that followed. He had been a member of the Lion Walk church and one of its trustees, but he had been 'worried away'[160] from that church, presumably because of a disagreement with those who were trying to oust Herrick. Francis had listened instead to Herrick's preaching, and in April 1842 he became a member at Stockwell.[161] Four days after the ejection, Francis and Thomas Green met at J.S. Barnes' office to try and reach an agreement. Francis and Green could never accept the validity of the mortgage, and things were at an impasse. In the end, they had to accept an unjust figure of £650 as the debt owed, and this time Barnes agreed they could pay it.[162]

Herrick preached in the Bible Room in Lion Walk while Stockwell Chapel was cleaned and prepared for use again. The Baptists also kindly offered the use of their chapel in the evening. Herrick preached very topical sermons. At the Bible Room a packed congregation heard a sermon on Acts 8:1, 'at that time there was a great persecution against the church which was at Jerusalem ...' At the Baptist Chapel Herrick likened the situation to that in Nehemiah's time, with the question that great man had asked: 'shall such a man as I flee?' The courage of the man stood out for the whole town to see.

By April 2, 1843, the congregation were back in Stockwell Chapel, and soon church members and congregation began to put their names down to pay off the debt. Some of the ladies had already started work on this. One of the local diarists tells us:[163]

Miss Posford waited upon me for a contribution to raise the fund for redeeming Mr Herrick's chapel called 'Stockwell Chapel' from the hands of the Mortgagees, when I gave her sixpence. There is a party of ladies who have undertaken to go from door to door the town through on the same errand ...

At the same time, there were those who were trying to blacken Herrick's name. Mr S.A. Phillbrick, who was related to Morris's wife, lent the same diarist, William Wire, incriminating papers:[164]

Mr S A Phillbrick lent me some Mss, squibs relating to the affair of unroofing the Old Chapel in Helens Lane, in consequence of a dispute between the pastor (Rev. J

185

Herrick) and the members of the church ...

So many people act on the worldly assumption: there is 'no smoke without fire.' Herrick suffered from this assumption all the time he was at Stockwell Chapel, and its injustice has prevented the rehabilitation of his name even today.

The progress of collecting money to pay off the debt was very encouraging. In June 1843, Herrick recorded in the minute book:[165]

> Since the last church meeting £450 has been received on account of the chapel debt and the whole £650 paid to our oppressors, £150 being borrowed of Mr Samuel Blomfield, who gave £50 as did Mr Francis and J H £52. It is hoped that £50 more will come in shortly from the collecting books which have hitherto done well.

By the end of August, the chapel had been tastefully spruced up on the outside, and the money to pay for it collected straightaway: debt would be a thing of the past. What rejoicing there was in the Spring of 1844! Here, in bold letters, is the inscription in the minute book:

Never again would Stockwell Chapel be in debt—God had delivered them from all their fears and all their enemies.

The start of the third Congregational Church in Colchester

Herrick's enemies were very quick off the mark, once Herrick had the keys of Stockwell Chapel again, and it was evident that the debt would be paid off. It was only May 12, 1843 when David Morris held his first open meeting. Before this, the originators of a third Independent church:[166]

deliberated long and sought Divine counsel guidance before any *public* display was made of their intentions.

David Morris's group were all clear that the principal difficulty lay in the lack of a suitable place to meet. They did not mention, of course, that they had failed to take over Stockwell Chapel, but their next target was interesting, the Old Meeting Room in Helens Lane, then occupied by a few Swedenborgians. They were very soon put off by its dilapidated state and had to look elsewhere. They ended up building their own chapel in Headgate Street.

There were very few of Stockwell Chapel's members who joined Headgate. George Lester, one of Herrick's early friends, but greatest opponents at the end, tried it out. He joined them at their first communion in August 1843 but seems not to have become a member. Only three other Stockwell men can be traced to Headgate: Lester's brother-in-law, John Vale, Joseph Williams and James Roy. This probably indicates that the sort of agenda the new church was offering had little appeal to Stockwell Chapel people.

God's purpose in the trials at Stockwell Chapel in the 1840s

When severe trials come upon a Christian, it is not always possible to discover the reasons why the all-sovereign God should have allowed them. In such circumstances, we fall back on Romans 8:28, 'And we know that all things work together for good to those who love God, to those who are the called according to His purpose.' In Herrick's case, I think there is less of a mystery; God's kind hand can be discerned more clearly. Two major benefits came from these events:

1. Herrick was put under the Lord's chastening hand. This had a purifying effect upon him, for that is God's purpose in allowing it: Hebrews 12:11, 'Now no chastening seems to be joyful for the present, but painful; nevertheless, afterward it yields the peaceable fruit of righteousness to those who have been trained by it.' Herrick's books written at this period show that he most definitely benefited from the discipline.

2. Church members with no sympathy for the saving gospel that was preached at Stockwell, finally left the church in peace. It is interesting that the years of trial were actually the years of greatest numerical blessing, the details of which we will cover in the next chapter.

Chapter 11
Quieter years at Stockwell Chapel; trials at home

The last 22 years of Herrick's ministry were notable for their lack of major church incidents. Quietness is not always good for the soul. The Scriptures tell how king Asa flourished when a million Ethiopians threatened to overwhelm his kingdom; but in his old age after many years of peace, he neglected to seek the Lord in his illness, preferring the advice of the doctors. The Lord knows what is best for each of his servants, so it was with Joseph Herrick. God sent trials as well as blessings during his last years in Colchester, but there is no doubt that Herrick came to his grave in peace.

Church blessings in 1843

1843 was a remarkable year for Herrick. We have seen how anxious he was during the coup attempt and its eventual failure, but there were encouragements too, as soon as they were back in Stockwell Chapel. In April, more people were present at the Lord's Supper (180) than for at least three years. Herrick adds a prayer to the minute book entry:[167]

> Thus we begin afresh. May peace now prevail and prosperity be granted unto us for Christ's sake!

What a relief it must have been when church meetings *were* held in peace, and the Lord's presence was felt. A month later Herrick could speak of a calm and gracious meeting where one member could say,[168] 'Surely God was in this place!' Before their return to Stockwell, the church had had all the disadvantages of meeting in the Bible room in Lion Walk. How encouraging it was in September to discover that the Lord had blessed His word to the salvation of one of the listeners during this time of deep trouble.[169]

At the end of 1843, Herrick could report:[170]

The year has been one of unusual increase, 39 having been added, and appearances promise much usefulness. May he who has carried thus far mercifully through the most trying year the Church and its Minister have known, avert evil and increase good. The minister will complete the 30th year of his service on the 23rd and if health continues till then, without having been out of the pulpit a single Sabbath in all that time. Laus Dei! (Praise be to God!)

1843 turned out to be the most fruitful year of Herrick's ministry, judged by the number of new members joining the church that year. How kind and good of God to temper trials with blessing!

Church meetings modified to minimise friction

From the very beginning, church meetings had been held on the Friday evening before the Lord's Day when the Lord's Supper was shared together. The main purpose of this meeting was to prepare the hearts of the Lord's people for this solemn yet joyful remembrance. Sadly, over the years, this had been lost sight of, as arguments took place about the suitability of new candidates, and later, strife concerning the trust deeds and the deacons' roles. The church had recognised how divisive such arguments could be, and as early as 1828 had resolved that if differences could be anticipated then special church meetings should be arranged, rather than disturb preparation for the Lord's Day.[171] Even this modification had not been enough, so that in 1832 it was decided that elder Brethren of the church should examine all candidates *privately*, and only present to the church meeting cases where admission was very likely.[172] This last change had been reversed during the deacon struggles of 1839; a case of the deacons wanting to eliminate all ministerial involvement and wrest all control into their hands. The final alteration to the method of receiving members was made in the temporary peace of 1841 when all members, male and female, agreed to Herrick's proposal:[173]

> It will perhaps be best from this day forward, not to appoint visitors when candidates are proposed. It is as much the duty of one member as another to interest himself about those who may come forward, and therefore I propose mentioning them, and leaving their names for a month, as usual. If any object, they can let me know; if any like to converse with them, they can do so; and, at the month's end, if no serious objection is made, that they be admitted by vote as usual.

It is noticeable that, after all these sensible changes, many more people were involved with the 'selection process,' yet apart from one case in 1846, argument was kept away from the church meeting itself.

The final change Herrick made was in the way he encouraged church members prior to the Lord's Supper. In the beginning this had been a short exhortation from the scripture with no fixed plan. By 1830 he had started to read extracts from Puritan books. The list of books he read from reflects the breadth of his own study: Flavel, Charnock, Howe, Gurnall, Cotton Mather, Doolittle, Erskine. Lengthy portions were sometimes read:[174]

> A long and beautiful extract from Erskine on 'What think ye of Christ?' was read by the Minister.

The minister clearly enjoyed the reading, but the thoughts were way beyond some of the church members. In November 1844, a new way of doing things was introduced:[175]

> The practice of reading an extract was this evening given up, a wish having been expressed that the pastor should speak, and he commenced with Matt 26:17–19, intending to go through in all the gospels, expounding the parts relating to the Lord's Supper, in the same way that the Psalms are gone over on Monday evening.

Herrick listened to his church members and was humble enough to suit his ministry to their capacity. He began by expounding the last chapters of Matthew, followed it with comments in equivalent passages in the three other gospels, and finally dipped into the seven churches of Asia at the very end of his ministry. How interesting it would be to have copies of these devotional expositions.

Joys and trials in family life

One of Ann and Joseph's chief joys was to see their children saved and added to the church fellowship. The eldest child Ann was 18 at the time of her coming into membership, well before the troubles of 1839 to 1843. The minute book describes Herrick's feelings:[176]

> This evening Miss Herrick … was admitted (unanimously) into the Church. It was a very impressive season, and especially because of the admission of the minister's daughter, and the interesting letters of hers which her father read.

Herrick had to endure some severe trials with his son John Douglas. John seems to have been a typically rebellious youth, and a sorrow to his parents. Drink was a source of problems at one stage. John Herrick, and John Hignell his friend, were once invited to the chapel anniversary celebrations and play in a game of cricket. Joseph Blomfield, writing in 1914 remembers:[177]

> as their luggage cab contained other things than bats and wickets and were pitched and caught between each other with the corks in, they were not invited a second time.

Herrick made every attempt to help his son and managed to set him up in the grocery business. John's warehouse was right next to Joseph and Ann's residence at 12 North Hill, Colchester, and he specialised in all manner of quite exotic cheeses in addition to the usual fare.

Disaster struck at three o'clock in the morning of Sunday, 23rd November 1845. A fire broke out in John's storeroom: all the materials, particularly the cheeses were highly combustible, and the adjoining houses were almost entirely of wooden construction. The newspaper reported that the fire:[178]

> … threatened the destruction of the Rev. Joseph Herrick's dwelling-house adjoining, as well as the whole range of houses on the east side of North Hill. Four engines from the Colchester Fire Office, were promptly at the spot … The flames first raged with great fury … but there being fortunately an excellent supply of water from two wells nearby, and from the tank belonging to the fire office, the four engines were at play upon the flames in about quarter of an hour after their arrival, and although Mr. Herrick's house was not of brick, nor the houses adjoining, the firemen through their active exertions, succeeded in confining the flames to Mr. H's house … danger to the adjoining houses was at an end, and before six o'clock the fire was entirely got under. Part of the stock of grocery is

saved; but the Rev. Mr. Herrick's extensive library is much damaged. Part of the furniture is also saved. The house is nearly gutted, and the damage is roughly calculated at about £1,200 ... The origin of the fire is enveloped in mystery ... The fire was first discovered by a young woman named Ellen Clover, who was asleep in bed in an adjoining house to the warehouse, and was awoke by the snapping of the flames, upon which she ran down stairs into the street in her night clothes, and gave the alarm, or in all probability several lives would have been lost.

Did a disastrous fire prevent Herrick from preaching later that Sunday morning? Not a bit of it! Blomfield records:[179]

He was in his pulpit on Sunday morning to the minute, and had to explain that the very coat he was preaching in he had to borrow, I think, from Mr Newell opposite.

Figure 11: North Hill In 2015, No 12 a few houses below the church

The fire was a severe trial to both father and son. John was very soon declared bankrupt, and so was dragged through the courts eight months later. With all his account books destroyed in the conflagration he was expected to give a detailed inventory of the cheeses which were left, their value, and from whom they had been bought. John, for years, found it difficult to find long term employment, and he had a growing family to care for. Much prayer was offered by the church on his behalf. Prayer was answered and John was converted and accepted into church membership in 1851. The minute book, written by his father describes the joy of the occasion:[180, 181]

> This evening … the minister's son, John Douglas Herrick, once a great sorrow, many prayers offered by the Church for him, and many eyes wet this evening on his account. May he grow in grace, and become a devoted servant of Christ …

> … Many were affected at the reading of part of J D H's letter, and many prayers were offered for him and for all. O, for an abundant answer …

We cannot trace all John's struggles to find employment, but we can see the trauma his troubles created in the family from Herrick's diary written in 1858, then 13 years after the fire. The news of John's continued problems surfaced early in January, greatly worrying his father. At this point, John was married, with a fourth child about to be born. Joseph could see his son becoming nothing more than a beggar, and who would look after the grandchildren? Numerous letters and donations were sent by post, so it was an even greater shock one Sunday in August to find out that John was still in great distress in London, and all this came to his notice just half an hour before he was due to preach! Just eight days later, Herrick discovered from a letter that John was starving in Bristol, selling oatmeal! Much prayer went up to God in heaven, and those prayers were answered speedily. By the end of 1858 John was settled in Birmingham as a fully employed Cork Sock Manufacturer, and the fourth grandchild was safely delivered in that city. Herrick recorded his last diary entry:

> This a year which has been very quiet, but very chequered in its experience. Alienation of daughter; removal of John to Bristol without consulting me; loss of a number of hearers by death and removal etc. Ends in more mercy than could well be expected. O Lord, help and save! And accept gratitude for what of mercy is mingled with all!

We do not know why Herrick was alienated from his daughter as well as having problems with John, but it is evident that he also found the consequences of the fire difficult to deal with, and family conflict may have sprung up as a result. As early as 1827, Herrick had made a will, with the help of the solicitor Samuel Wittey: still a friend at this stage. It is clear from this document that Herrick would have a share in substantial property. Part of this was inherited by Ann from the Douglas side of the family; some was promised by covenant to Joseph from Rev. Archibald Douglas, Ann Herrick's uncle. All the land and buildings were in Springfield, to the east of Chelmsford, about 20 miles from Colchester.

The 1827 will was well written, but because of changes in his family, and as a result of the fire, it needed to be modified. Unwisely, Herrick took it upon himself to rewrite it. Herrick should really have learned from his experience with the chapel trust deeds that formulating legal niceties was not his forte. The will he wrote in December 1845 and then rewrote a year later was inadequate. After his death, there was a tooth and nail battle over the division of his property between the childless married daughter and the son with three boys and three girls to feed. A substantial amount of income came from these rented properties, but at the death of Ann and John, the whole estate of Joseph Herrick was sold in 1896,[182] with the children of John Douglas presumably benefiting.

It must be said that Herrick's problems in the early years of his ministry made him distrustful of anybody, even his own family members. Although a very loving and kind man, he sometimes acted as a control freak in family as well as church. It is not surprising that his children fell out with him, and this probably explains why so little care was taken to preserve his diaries and other effects, or to write an adequate biography of him. Not every Christian man is given a happy family, and Herrick certainly experienced many ups and downs in his.

Constant friends and a restored friend

The Blomfields, were a large farming family who could trace their ancestry back to the Normans and had settled in Essex in the mid-1600s. There were two main branches: one in Dedham, 8 miles north east of Colchester, the other in Greenstead on the eastern outskirts of Colchester. Herrick's chief friends from this family were three men, all Samuels, covering the entire period of his pastorate. They all seem to have been extremely loyal yet very humble men whom God put in place exactly when Herrick needed them.

The first and second Samuels were father and son from the farm in Greenstead. The first Samuel Blomfield was one of the earliest persons to be received into membership of the new chapel in 1817. Herrick could see that Samuel was a spiritual man and put his name forward for the diaconate in 1819. The church was ready, but Samuel felt otherwise, and only joined James Nash a year later when George Lester was also appointed. This man was very useful to the church, but sadly died in 1824.

The second Samuel Blomfield became one of Herrick's

mainstays during the attempt to oust him in the 1840s. A converted man, he was slow to ask for church membership. Herrick told of the reaction when his name was put forward in 1840:[183]

His parents were members, and long wished to see him take this step. He has long been taking an active and useful part among us in those things which our late pretended deacons neglected, and the members seemed much pleased that he was at length coming forward.

Like his father, Samuel became a deacon, then the church treasurer and church reader as well. He it was who handled all the financial matters for the church while the debt was being paid off in 1843–4, contributing generous amounts of money from his own business on the way. During the summer months Samuel offered the use of his barn and fields for the church Sunday School outing.[184] What a treat for 200 excited children, running free with 50 adults doing their best to keep things in control! When all the games were over, the youngsters would be regaled with tea and cakes, in a barn decorated with flowers and evergreens, and then demonstrate how well they could do their recitations.

The third Samuel Blomfield (1800–1875) is described by Sier as:[185]

A farmer at Hazleton's farm and one of the chief supporters of the Rev. Joseph Herrick.
He lived at Dedham and was probably a member of the church there under William Crathern. This explains why his name cannot be traced in the list of members at Stockwell chapel, though we know he listened regularly to Herrick's preaching. It was providential that the home in Dedham was far enough away from Colchester to become a welcome

retreat, a sort of oasis in the desert of intrigue and struggle, both during the Unitarian crisis and in the deacon rebellion 25 years later. This Samuel was just six years younger than Joseph and outlived him; he remained a good friend for the whole time Herrick was in Colchester.

Samuel Blomfield kept a diary, and a few of his comments during the 1840s show where his sympathies lay:[186]

1840, April 10 'Rev. Herrick dined and spent the afternoon here. Attended meeting at Stockwell Chapel vestry when the chapel was agreed to be mortgaged!!'

1843, Feb 19 'Attended Stockwell Chapel perhaps for the last time'

1843, Feb 21 'Stockwell Chapel shut up this forenoon'

1843, April 2 'Re-opening of Stockwell Chapel after being shut up by our enemies, 5 Sundays'

The value which this Samuel Blomfield put on his friendship with Herrick is demonstrated by a long poem he wrote on a folded card for a celebration of Herrick's 50th Jubilee in Colchester:[187]

A few thoughts upon the Jubilee of our beloved Pastor's ministry

Fifty summers, autumns, winters,
God has shown a gracious care;
Granted us a special blessing,
When you made your entrance here.

2 Earliest recollections cheer us,
You were then our choicest Friend,
And such friendship is enduring,
It indeed should never end.

3 Like your loving precious Master,
Your regard for us has been,
Through the sharpest tribulation,
Your affection has been seen.

4 Nothing less than holy influence,
Could have borne above the wave;
Who could then have cheered, supported,
But one infinite to save.

5 Like a warrior armed for battle,
You have stood with sword in hand;
And pushed forward in the conflict,
Pointed to the heavenly land.

6 O how oft the broken-hearted
Have received the healing word;
You have dealt out choicest blessings
From a loving tender Lord.

7 And the arrow of conviction,
As directed from above,
Led the sinner, humbled, weeping,
To a Saviour full of love.

8 Sinners who have long rejected,
Shut their ears to mercy's sound;
Even such have been arrested -
They the bleeding Lamb have found.

9 Let the thought of souls converted
Cheer and animate you now;
Many reached the heights of glory;
At their Saviour's feet they bow.

10 Many years may we be favoured
Still to hear your voice proclaim,
There, a blessed full salvation:
Grace is found in Jesus' name.

11 Trials many you have passed through,
Trials which your people share;
But the crown of life resplendent
You as conqueror shall wear.

12 May the comfort you have tendered
Now return into your heart,
In the Saviour's love and blessing
Live and grow and never part.

13 And when this frail life is ended,
Join the blessed Choir above,
With a numerous number enter;
There to share a Saviour's love.

14 Then how sweet to gaze and wonder
On a Saviour's loving breast;
Bless the kind and loving Jesus,
Who secured this heavenly rest.

15 All the mystery unravelled,
Why we met so much to pain;
Why we were so sad so troubled,
This blest light will then explain.

16 Darkness, doubt and grief o'ershadow
All our path while travelling here;
We look up and faith assures us:
There's a bright and happier sphere.

17 Our dear Pastor, people, Teachers;
Children, may we share this bliss;
Spend a long and blest forever,
Where the dear Redeemer is.

Let Christian regard cast a veil over all that is incorrect and accept these few lines as breathings from the heart.'

I have assigned this poem to Samuel Blomfield, but there is no signature to make it certain. He is by far the most likely author. James Nash knew him for the whole time too, but his fall-out in the 1840s would make such a heartfelt response hypocritical if not impossible.

This a very revealing poem. It shows the real fruitfulness of Herrick's gospel preaching. It also shows the reality of the trials he went through and how his true friends reacted to them. The warmth of genuine Christian love shines through these lines, especially the empathy shown by the sharing of verse 11 and the repeated 'we' in the 15th stanza. Herrick, for all his faults, was capable of attracting real affection from his friends.

I must finish this section by drawing attention to Herrick's earliest friend—James Nash. This poor man had been a pawn in the hand of ruthless operators, especially his son-in-law John Stuck Barnes. Herrick recognised this, I think, and attempted as early as 1841 to make overtures of friendship again. These were rebuffed at first. This is the record in the minute book:[188]

The minister mentioned what had been done in the case of Mr Nash. Mr Green had conversed with him, but thought him as hostile as ever, and therefore gave up the object, especially as he found on getting a person to watch him at the Collection for incidentals, when he did not put anything into the plate, nor has he paid for his pew for 2 years or more, etc., all which shows there is no hope of his being brought to a better mind at present.

How many other attempts were made we do not know, but how wonderful to find this entry 15 years later:[189]

> A damp thick day and evening, but moderate meeting. Interesting however from Mr James Nash, 86, who has been away from us for 16 or 17 years, being reinstated as a communicant.

Interesting indeed! Nor was this all: one of the final entries in Herrick's own diary on Christmas day 1858 reads:

> Called on Mr Nash.

This small phrase speaks volumes: it tells of the wonder of forgiveness; Christians united again in fellowship. How heart-warming to evidence the reality of Christian grace leading to godly behaviour! James Nash died at the age of 93, giving him seven years of renewed friendship with the saints at Stockwell chapel.

Chapter 12
Assessing Herrick's writing

Unitarians and ''Immanuel'

The first book of Herrick's that we can examine is his response to the Unitarian crisis in 1815–1816: 'Immanuel.' His motives for writing this book, and the style he uses reveal much about the character of the man. In Herrick's script, you will never find dry theological dissertation on the doctrine of the Trinity. His purpose is not to display his knowledge or to impress his readership. He tells us in the Preface:[190]

> My book is particularly intended for plain people. There are many books upon this subject which are above the generality of understandings. My aim therefore has been, to state the truth as it is in Jesus, in the language of the Holy Scriptures ...

Herrick's book sets out to collect scriptures about the person and work of Christ, from Genesis to Revelation, with only cursory remarks upon them. He wishes above everything, to impress his readership of the *absolute certainty* of the Divinity of Christ and the *infinite effectiveness* of the atonement he made at Calvary for all who believe. The sheer number of scriptures he quotes has a cumulative power of conviction, so much so that this reader wondered at the end how anyone could have a moment's doubt.

What lifts this book above the ordinary, however, is the application. Herrick writes his book as a series of 25 letters to a friend. This is an old style of writing, not unusual for the time. What makes it different in Herrick's case is the growing conviction that this friend is *a real person,* not an imaginary man with imaginary differences of opinion. How plainly and honestly, he deals with him! How earnestly he pleads with him to consider the scriptures and turn from the folly of his unbelief! A few examples will demonstrate his searching application.

At the end of the fifth letter on passages in Deuteronomy, he deals with the pride found among Unitarians:[191]

You seem to wonder how you can be wrong, with so many great names on your side. You will soon understand why many great men have taken the side of heterodoxy. 'The world by wisdom knew not God.' Gospel truth is far above the understanding of the mere natural man, be he ever so learned. One of its first requirements is to renounce self absolutely, and for ever ... above all say, are not these truths more suited to my condition as a sinner than the notions I have imbibed?

At the finish of the 14th letter on the last chapters of Isaiah, he reasons with him about separating from his unbelieving compatriots:[192]

O my friend, there is great comfort in Christ. Come to him, cleave to him, depend upon him, delight in him; and though you may be despised for it by some, and hated and cast out by others, remember, 'He shall appear to your joy, and they shall be ashamed,' Isaiah 66:5, 11, 12, 13.

As Herrick begins in the New Testament he urges his friend not to trust in the power of reason, but to bow to the revealed word of God alone:[193]

Remember in how many instances you have needed the advice of others because your own reason was not sufficient to direct you: and if this has been the case in worldly matters, how presumptuous must it be to resort to reason as your only guide in Divine things?

Herrick's anxiety for his friend grows stronger, notably with this impassioned plea at the end of the 20th letter concerning passages in Mark and Luke:[194]

My own confidence seems strengthened by every letter I write to you: but this will not content me. I long to see you freed from your sceptical notions and infidel prejudices. I am glad if you feel any sense of the excellence of Christianity; but, alas! My brother, we may admire it as a system of morals till we die, and yet remain so utterly alienated in heart from God, as to be beyond the possibility of ever seeing his face. I am anxious for your present and future happiness; and I know that nothing can secure it but an interest in the obedience and blood of the despised Nazarene. Ah! My dear friend, your notions will not bear you out. In the end, the foundation on which you have been building will totter; and all those fine speculations with which you have been amused, will fly away as the chaff of the summer threshing-floors. Say, O say, I beseech you, can you stand before a holy God, and plead innocence? No. You are guilty. If so, then, on what ground do you expect pardon? God is merciful. O! Fallacious dependence. Is he not also just? How then shall his justice be satisfied? If mercy is ever exercised towards you, it must be in a way that is consistent with the strictest justice; and, if so, it can only be exercised through Him who presented his body as a sheath to the sword of Divine justice, that the poor, repenting believing sinner, might be righteously pardoned. May you, through grace, believe and be justified from all things freely, through the blood of him who of God is made unto us, wisdom, and righteousness, and sanctification, and redemption. Amen.

One more quote from this book is sufficient to demonstrate Herrick's unusually powerful spiritual application. In my estimation, Herrick stands on the same level as A.W. Pink in his close dealing with his readers. The one difference is that, in Herrick's case, he remained as pastor of a local church, while most of Pink's writing was from the 'safety' of his study with none but his readers to worry about. Here is his comment at the end of his letter dealing with Acts:[195]

Your embracing the sentiments you now profess, did not, I know, originate from the careful study of the scriptures, but from an unsettledness of mind, arising from the want of an experimental knowledge of the gospel. This made you entertain with readiness anything that came with the charm of novelty. You read; you then went to hear; you drank the insidious, the intoxicating, the deadly narcotic: your proud heart scorned the humiliating gospel of Jesus; you vaunted yourself on having discovered a new path to glory and to happiness: (and oh! how affected was I when I heard it!) you exulted in the discovery that Christ was no more than yourself! But, alas! My friend, how have you sometimes felt since then? Conscience raves at times; trials oppress you; Satan urges you to greater zeal in his cause: you proceed; you reflect; you anticipate; and, ah! What then? —Ah! you dread; you pause and say, what if all should not be right? What if the New Testament is true and those passages are not all interpolations, which speak of Christ's Deity? What if those passages which Socinians tell me are not rightly translated should be found correct: ah! What then? What? My dear friend; why, you are lost. You, like Balaam, will behold Christ but not nigh. You will be tormented without end at an awful distance from all that can give happiness!

Let these truths weigh upon your mind as their

importance deserves. Read the New Testament for yourself, with frequent and earnest prayer for instruction. And my sincere prayer is that you may know Jesus as your Saviour and your God. Amen.

Herrick's book Immanuel seems to have had a very limited print run; its truths and searching gospel application deserve to be better known, but, alas! the author knows of only two copies of the book, in Colchester library. If any doubt remained about Herrick's behaviour during his early years at Helens Lane, his book Immanuel leaves us absolutely clear as to his motives. Here is a man deeply concerned about the dangers of Unitarianism, pleading with those who are inclined to lower Jesus Christ to a mere man, warning them of the terrible danger they are in. To Herrick, the battle for souls in 1816 was a matter of spiritual life or death. The crisis was not primarily caused by a clash of personalities, nor was it materially worsened by the irritability of a very young and inexperienced pastor. Rather it was the result of a collision between a man who was all out for the authentic Biblical gospel and a minority of his enemies who firmly believed that they had *inherited* 'grace' and 'church position' from their forebears of many decades before, even though they held entirely different and heretical views which denied both the Deity of Christ and His atoning sacrifice at Calvary! It is astonishing to realise how few Christians in Colchester recognised the danger of compromising with Unitarians. Even true believers treated them with exaggerated respect as fellow Dissenters. It took a man of Herrick's deep convictions to deal almost single-handedly with the problem and root it out. Yet we see in Immanuel how lovingly and faithfully he deals with those with whom he differed. Herrick stands out as a man with a pastor's heart: both a Mr Valiant for Truth and a Mr Greatheart.

Indifference to the gospel and 'The Monitory Mirror'

17 years later, with a much-enlarged experience of the human heart, Herrick turned his attention to a matter that is of great concern to any preacher: the *indifference* of so many hearers to the claims of the gospel. In the Victorian era it was possible to preach the Bible even with approval from high places. There are grave dangers when Christianity is fashionable; Herrick describes some of them in his introduction to his next book, the Monitory Mirror:[196]

In this age of liberality and refinement 'the offence of the cross' has in some degree ceased. Religion basks in the sunshine of prosperity ... we have too much reason to fear, that thousands are satisfying themselves with the mere shadow of religion.

There are not wanting books and sermons which describe an easy religion and present a flattering portrait of the human character. To these many refer and are deceived. They make a false estimate of themselves and are thereby exposed to ruin.

Herrick tackles the problem of spiritual indifference head on. With the Bible as his mirror, he first pictures the ugliness of indifference: what he calls the *marks* or we would call the symptoms. He follows this with a Biblical diagnosis of the soul's condition: the *causes* of this spiritual disease. The next chapter gives a serious warning about the *consequences* of indifference. In the final section, as a good physician of souls, Herrick displays the medicine of God's word which we must apply if we would be restored: what he calls the *means of recovery*.

The title of Herrick's book will never be a page-turner: it gives little indication of the subject he is dealing with. Leaving this aside, the writing shows all the close dealing with the conscience we saw in his earlier 'Immanuel.' The application is as much to backsliding believers as it is to the unconverted. The sub-headings relating to the symptoms of indifference make this very clear:[197]

1. A dislike of religious conversation.
2. An aversion to faithful books and sermons, which probe the conscience and character.
3. Irregularity of attendance upon the public ordinances of religion.
4. Mixing much and unnecessarily with ungodly company.
5. The neglect of family worship.
6. The omission of secret prayer, is, perhaps, after all, the most decisive mark of indifference.

One of the chief means Herrick uses to engage with his readers is by means of little sketches, with names which remind us of the characters Bunyan uses in *Pilgrim's Progress*. Reviewers of the book commented very favourably on this feature, when it was first published.

Most of the sketched characters are real people Herrick had met, and he uses their history to warn all who are tempted along the path of apostacy. The problems associated with characters such as Mr Sleepy, Mrs Gadabout, Mr Timid, Mr Indulgence and Mr Deceiveself need no commentary here, but Herrick also has an interesting character called Mr Public who hardly ever prays in secret but is often on his feet in the prayer meeting, under the impression that he has gift in this capacity. Mr Sullen reacts badly whenever any trials come along, while Mr Stoutheart pacifies his conscience whenever he is tempted to indulge his darling sin. We leave this excellent book with the heartfelt tale of Mr Newman: his going astray and his restoration:[198]

Mr. Newman was a converted character; and, for a long time, lived so as to adorn his profession. His heart was warmed with love, his soul burned with zeal for God, and his house was a resort for God's ministers and people. He prospered in business ... He journeyed often into distant counties ... he was a wise man, and his judgment was much thought of, even when comparatively young, and, at one time, he was so taken up with business that he had, when at home, no time for those family exercises in which he formerly delighted so much, but which had, of course, been interrupted by his frequent and long absences. Indeed, he had learned to do without them when journeying, and felt their need the less when at home. But this was not all. He had been led into many improprieties of conduct, and, through habits formed by association, he began to do in many things as ungodly men did. He began now to be often absent from his family of an evening, when he might have been with them; and frequently from his place of worship on the Lord's day, a thing which formerly he very much disliked. In a word, he became indifferent in religion; and though he was still always kind to the ministers of religion, and his guinea was always ready when wanted for the cause of God, good men who had long known him mourned over him, and some of them even ventured to hint to him how he had fallen; but others, who were often at his table, because he was bountiful, rather soothed and flattered him than otherwise; and he, though he sometimes betrayed a consciousness of the change which had come over him, always seemed easier when he had said, as he frequently did, 'Business now swallows me up, so that I cannot do as I formerly did, but I do the best I can.'

Thus things remained, till God was pleased deeply to affect his heart by a very solemn discourse on those words of the prophet, 'Ephraim is joined to idols: let him alone,' Hosea 4:11. This, concurring with some domestic afflictions,—or rather God's Holy Spirit concurring with these,—completely aroused him from the torpid state into which he had sunk. And never can his Christian friends forget how deeply he was affected, how speedily he reformed, and how full and free he was in acknowledging his offences, and how ardently he adored God for sparing him to hear that sermon, and to see the error of his ways. The joy of his soul now seemed to exceed what he felt on his conversion to God many years before, for he was now much more capable of justly appreciating the greatness of his mercy than then: it seemed to him a second spiritual birth, a new and overwhelming discovery of Divine love, and it filled him 'with joy unspeakable and full of glory.' He soon abandoned the sins which had led him astray, ceased to visit some who had been a snare to him, restored the worship of God in his family, became peculiarly cautious of his words and actions, and is now living in the enjoyment of the blessings of real devotedness to God, high in the esteem of his pastor and friends, and is very useful in comforting distressed consciences, and counselling and cautioning the young and the unstable, having himself known much of the devices of Satan. He views himself as 'a brand plucked out of the fire,' and is anxious to show his gratitude for so great a mercy.

How happy is Mr. Newman now, compared with what he would have been had he stifled his convictions and determined to turn to God at some future period, as many in similar circumstances have strangely promised!

Sinners in despair and 'Salvation possible to the vilest sinners'

Just at the point when Herrick was going through the fearful turmoil of the four-year plot to oust him from Stockwell chapel, we find him writing on a subject of vital importance to his hearers. The first problem he noticed was the sense of despair some of them felt of ever being saved. He describes them in the preface of his book: 'The greatness of God's mercy in Christ, or salvation possible to the vilest sinners.' Published in London, Ipswich and Colchester in 1842:

> Without being now, or having been formerly, enormously wicked, in open act, or regular habit, men may have … an overwhelming sense of the difficulties in the way of their salvation …

His prayer was that any who were tempted to despair would find relief by reading and praying over the sections of his book and especially after reading the many scriptures included.

We have seen Herrick's skill in drawing the reader in. He uses a quite different technique to achieve this in his 'Salvation,' book. He begins with a dialogue between himself (A) and the troubled enquirer (B). This is how the dialogue starts:[199]

> A. Ah, my dear friend, how do you do? I have not seen you for some time. I trust all is well with you.

> B. I wish it were so: but I fear it is not.

> A. How mean you? for though your countenance is clouded you appear in tolerable health.

> B. Well, as to the body, I have not much to complain of, although I fear that is not in a very good state: but my mind is dark, and is harassed, almost continually, with dismal,

214

unbelieving, and, at times, very horrid thoughts.

The depth of the poor man's despair is then very effectively described:[200]

I well remember that you used to tell me not to rely on frames and feelings; for that they might prove delusive and had done so to many; and that one promise or doctrine of holy scripture was worth more, and would one day weigh more, than all feelings and fancies. I have been under delusion. I never had any religion. I have not been a hypocrite exactly, perhaps: a hypocrite knowingly pretends to be what he is not, and designs to deceive others. I do not think I did so: but I have been deceived. I took education for conviction, and habit for conversion; and good spirits for clear evidence of grace and the light of God's countenance; and believed my soul reconciled because it was in peace. But, O, sir, how easy it is to delude one's-self, when the mind is strong, the hands fully occupied, the health good, and death seemingly far off; to what it is when the spirits are low, and all things seem against us! I once thought well of my state and was accustomed to speak rather confidently than doubtingly; now I fear that I am utterly destitute of sound religious hopes. What to do I know not. All seems dismal. Scripture looks dark, ordinances are no longer profitable to me, or enjoyed by me; and prayer brings no comfort—no nearness to God.

Herrick deals with the problem in masterly fashion. He proposes and comments on ten propositions:
1 God is inconceivably holy, and man is exceedingly vile,
2 The scheme of redemption evidently supposes the condition of man, if left to himself, to be irreparable,
3 Christ came to remedy all man's misery; and he is able to do all that he has undertaken,

4 No case is mentioned in the Bible as being beyond the power of the grace of our Saviour, Jesus Christ,

5 The scripture account of the divine nature, and the whole system of divine government, both spiritual and providential, teach that God delights in mercy,

6 The gift of Christ, 'that unspeakable gift,' ought to be, and is by itself a sufficient proof of God's all-surpassing mercy to man,

7 After all God has done to secure salvation to men, and to convince them of its possibility, to conclude that salvation is, in any case, impossible, is to suppose one of the three things following, a) That we have sinned beyond the extent of the merits of Jesus Christ and the mercies of God in and through him, or b) That notwithstanding all the Bible has said, there are peculiarities in our own case, which shut us out from salvation, or c) That God is insincere, and has held out hopes, invitations, and assurances, full, distinct, and positive, which yet mean nothing, and on which it would be unsafe to rely. Such reasonings are wrong: such conclusions are at variance with the whole scope of scripture; they are delusive, but, alas, common, because dictated by fear, guilt, and unbelief, which are common to all men,

8 The scripture cases of pardoned sinners show, very clearly, the possibility of enormous sins being forgiven,

9 Modern instances of the operation of divine grace show that there is no limit to the goodness and mercy of God in Christ,

10 The numerous texts of scripture that proclaim pardon, acceptance, and eternal life to every penitent believing sinner, abundantly sustain all that has been said in the preceding pages, and warrant every man, who longs to be saved, to close at once with the sincere offer of God in the gospel, of eternal happiness to all who come to him by

Jesus Christ.

Herrick's student clearly benefited from reading this book and confesses he has been rescued from the darkness, guilt, and misery, in which he then was sinking. He specially mentions the value he obtained from the views set before him, from the holy scriptures, *of the mercy of God in Christ.* Herrick shows us again his skill at applying scripture rather than arguing abstruse points of theology. He has this interesting comment in the concluding dialogue:[201]

If men would dispute less, and read and pray more, it would be a good thing, and much good would come of it to the Christian world. You know that, though not indifferent to truth, I have long looked upon disputation about the recondite and extreme meaning of Christian doctrines as unprofitable. Being upon this subject, I will tell you, just to show how much nearer good men of all parties are to each other than they think for, one of the very best anecdotes I ever met with, and which relates to the excellent Cornelius Winter. 'Mr. Winter was lately in company with an Arminian, who spoke violently against the doctrine of election. "You believe election," said Mr. Winter, "as firmly as I do." "I deny it," answered the other; "on the contrary, it is a doctrine I detest." "Do you believe that all men will be saved at the last day, or some only?" "Only some." "Do you imagine that those some will be found to have saved themselves?" "No, certainly: God in Christ is the only Saviour of sinners." "But God could have saved the rest, could he not?" "No doubt." "Then salvation is peculiar to the saved?" "To be sure." "And God saves them designedly, and not against his will?" "Certainly." "And willingly suffers the rest to perish, though he could easily have hindered it?" "It should seem so." "Then is not this election?" "It amounts to the same thing."

A book reviewer of the time had this to say of Herrick's book:

'An excellent piece of practical divinity, of the same stamp as Bunyan's Grace abounding.' *Christian Witness*.

High praise indeed.

Sanctification and 'The greatest sinners capable of being rendered holy and happy'

Another concern of Herrick in the 1840s was the number of faulty views of Christian sanctification being taught at the time, with the unhappiness of some true believers as a result. He mentions these incorrect views in the preface to his last book: 'Salvation certain and complete; or the greatest sinners capable of being rendered holy and happy:'

(Sanctification) is denied to have any reality by some; it is said to be instantaneous and never progressive by others; whilst a third party, and, alas! an increasing one, pronounces it to be the work of the priesthood—and not a few, denying, or not believing, the Deity and influences of the Holy Spirit, look upon all holiness, whether called regeneration or sanctification, to be the work of each individual in and upon himself.

This book was designed to be read in conjunction with the earlier volume on salvation. Its style is very similar, with introductory and final dialogues between Herrick and his student, the whole book written in Herrick's homely manner with plenty of illustrations from the created world. Herrick's object in writing is described:[202]

The design of this second publication is to show, that though sanctification is not in all cases alike ... yet it is a reality; and must, in the nature of things, and where there is time for it, be experienced; and that it must be progressive.

The necessity of progressive sanctification is powerfully presented, both from scripture and with examples from nature. The following example is typical:[203]

> Real religion will, and must, naturally and necessarily, · exert itself accordingly to its own proper nature. It cannot do otherwise, and it must produce holiness, as an apple tree must produce apples, if it produce at all. The bloom may be frozen and perish—or the winds may blow the blossom away before the fruit has set—the bark may be sickly—the root may be in a dead soil—the tree may not produce what it should, or under other and more favourable circumstances would; but it is an apple tree, and, under the worst circumstances, produces, in foliage, flower, and fruit, enough evidence of the fact; one apple is as decisive as a bushel: and if the quantity or quality be not what is approved, that is another affair, and may be remedied by removal, or by grafting, or by raising a new progeny from the seed … Nothing can show more clearly the essential holiness of the gospel of Christ than the language of St. Paul to the Thessalonians. "We are bound to give thanks alway to God for you, brethren, beloved of the Lord, because God hath from the beginning chosen you to salvation, through sanctification of the Spirit and belief of the truth: whereunto he called you by our gospel to the obtaining of the glory of our Lord Jesus Christ." 2 Thessalonians 2:13, 14.

The very useful section headings give an idea of the scope of this valuable work:
1 God is holy—*must* be so,
2 Whatsoever proceeds from a holy God *must* partake of his own nature,

3 Real religion, proceeding from a holy God, and being of a holy nature, *must* produce holy effects,

4 The Holy Spirit is the gracious and sovereign *Agent* employed in Sanctification,

5 The word of God is the principal *Instrument* by means of which Sanctification is carried on,

6 The ministers of the Gospel are instrumental in promoting holiness, and entirely by preaching Christ,

7 The trials of life do often promote Sanctification,

8 Bodily ailments are often made use of to advance Sanctification,

9 Sin is frequently overruled for increase of Sanctification,

10 Sanctimoniousness is not Sanctification,

11 Baptismal regeneration is not Sanctification,

12 Sanctification is not perfection.

A final point to make on this book is that it sheds invaluable light on the church troubles Herrick was going through at the time. The following conversation in the final dialogue is quite revealing:[204]

B. Ah, you have had much trial yourself, and are therefore able to feel for others. Thus, your master has qualified you "to speak a word in season to him that is weary." You have had some heavy trials of late.

A. Yes, very heavy; and from those I relied on as my own kindred, and whom I had uniformly endeavoured in every way to serve. It was cruel. But all were not equally blameworthy. They were led on by interested and unprincipled men. It is a long story and cannot be fully told as yet without pain to many, and that I shall avoid. O how I longed at times to be in a monastery, or a desert— anywhere to have done with the world, and with men ... But those feelings, I am happy to say, were not habitual.

Sometimes I could calmly leave all to Providence and live above man and all his littleness and malice.

B. It must, however, have been very painful to you, knowing yourself quite innocent of anything that deserved from your enemies the injuries they inflicted upon you.

A. Not near so painful as it would have been to know that I really deserved such treatment at their hands.

B. Why, no, assuredly. But still unmerited enmity, and undeserved reproach, are felt by all men to be very hard to bear with patience; at least so it has seemed with all I ever conversed with or read about.

A. And so I found in my experience. But I thought of what philosophy had done, and what religion ought to do far more effectually. If Plato could overlook, and scorn, and forget, the tyrant Dionysius, surely, I ought to endeavour to forget my enemies.

Herrick's hymn book

Herrick wrote a hymn book for his own congregation: a copy of the third edition published in 1836 is deposited in Dr Williams's library in London. Herrick had been used to writing in verse from his youth; hence his poetic sketches as well as his hymns. We saw one of his heart-felt hymns in Chapter 2, and there are quite a few of this character in the book. Herrick rarely soars to the skies in his hymnology: he was too down to earth for that. His hymns abound in application to gospel-needy sinners, and to believers needing to grow in the Christian life. What is missing are hymns that lift the soul to heaven, that rejoice in the promises and reach out to a glorious, all-sufficient Saviour and God. It is perhaps not surprising that none of them have ever been included in well-known hymn books. A selection of interesting examples is included in Appendix 2.

Chapter 13
Herrick's final days

Herrick in the 1850s

By the end of the 1850s, Herrick was showing distinct signs of old age. Although the church was in a peaceful state, family troubles were never far below the surface and his nerves, shattered by the conflict of the Unitarian period and the church property battles of the 1840s, began increasingly to trouble him. The tone of the diary of 1858 is much more sombre, with an old person's constant reference to the weather, but more worryingly, the low state of his mind. As a tenement owner at Springfield he was often vexed about financial matters and practical difficulties. He went so far as to say:

> The tenements ... have been such a snare to me ... I am at times sorely tried by trifles.

In spite of his feelings, God was gracious and helped him to rise above his circumstances when he came to God's house and rose to preach. A typical example of this is revealed in these comments in his diary:

> February 13 ... Very low at times about John and my territorial affairs, yet calm. Wet in evening and night ... Sunday February 14. Wet all day. Family attended for the day. Got above the day and my cares a good deal.

The melancholy note that tuned his heart for much of the 1850s, contrasts well with his Christian hope in the following poem, found loose in his diary:

JOSEPH HERRICK

Mile End, October 8, 1852

That old mill stands on the same green spot
Where it stood in days of yore;
But where are they who around it dwelt
When I was here before?
Alas! They are gone and times are changed;
Some are dead, and some are poor,
And have left the lands that once they tilled,
And shall hold farm land no more.
By folly and waste are some brought low;
And some by faults not their own;
But sickness, oppression and sin came here,
And those I once knew are gone.
Some to far distant lands have fled;
Some serve who did long command;
Some are poor who once made sure to be rich
And above all toil of the land.
Such are the changes that everywhere
Meet those who long survive;
Time alters all—both men and things,
How wondrous that I am alive!

What mercies have marked the flying years,
What sins and griefs and cares!
And now I am almost alone
In a world of sins and snares.
Yet will I trust in Him who is the same,
Whilst all around proclaims the lot of man,
All glory be to His most holy name,
Who is still what He was when this world first began.

The contrast between mutable man and the unchanging God
is there for all to see. The difference is even more marked if we
look at the proposed book with its title on the other side of the

same slip of paper. The front page is as shown below.

Figure 12: Proposed new Herrick book planned around 1852

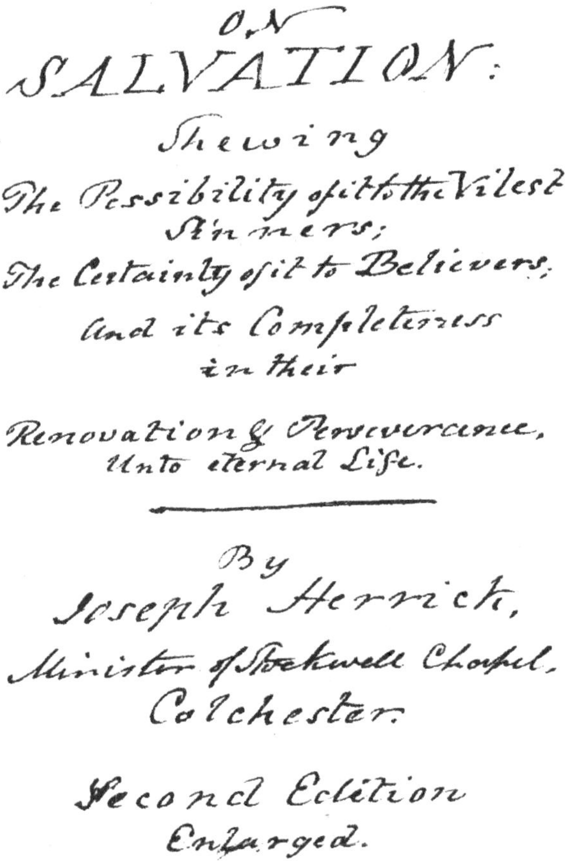

ON
SALVATION:

Shewing

The Possibility of it to the Vilest
Sinners;

The Certainty of it to Believers;

And its Completeness
in their

Renovation & Perseverance,
Unto eternal Life.

———

By
Joseph Herrick,
Minister of Stockwell Chapel,
Colchester.

Second Edition
Enlarged.

How uplifting to meditate on certainty, completeness, renovation and eternal life—all bought by a gracious Saviour for undeserving sinners living in a corrupt and changing world! We have no evidence that this book was ever published; but of the certainties it was to speak of, there is no doubt whatsoever.

The 1860s and the death of Ann Herrick

As the 1860s began, there were many more positive comments in the church minute book, more good meetings, and more people being brought into church fellowship.

In July 1862 Herrick lost the love of his life: his wife Ann. Never having a strong constitution, she suffered much from neuralgia at the end, and finally a stroke. Herrick commented of her: 'her end was peace.'[205] Joseph Blomfield, a young man at the time, tells us:[206]

> One of the strongest things, perhaps, he ever did was when he lost his own excellent wife, and because he said he knew her best, he stood and preached the funeral sermon himself.

When he was still a youth, he had expressed his love for Ann in a simple acrostic:[207]

A-dieu my dear Fair one adieu;
N-ow we for a season must part.
N-ay weep not—I'll not be untrue,

D-earest fair one I'll leave you my heart.
O-then you have nothing to fear,
U-nsettled I am not—but true.
G-o I may but my heart I leave here;
L-ovely Maid I'll love no one but you.
A-ccept this last kiss—and dear Maiden farewell;
S-oon I shall return and then all shall be well.

That affection for Ann was lasting, and the inscription on her tombstone is simple, but telling:

In affectionate remembrance of
Ann wife of
The Rev. J. Herrick
Who being meet for glory
Entered her rest on
July 14th, 1862
Aged 70 years

Joseph Herrick's death and funeral[208]

On Saturday January 21, 1865, Herrick conducted the funeral of one of his most respected church members: James Botton. The next day Herrick preached as usual at both Sunday services, though many noticed he was suffering from a slight cold. On Wednesday January 25, the chapel was open as usual for the Wednesday evening lecture, but to everyone's alarm, Herrick was not in attendance but at home in his bed. On Thursday bronchitis and severe breathing difficulties set it. Although on Friday the patient declared himself to be feeling better, this was not the judgment of the doctors in attendance. They advised all the family members to be contacted and make their way to the bedside as quickly as possible. Herrick's illness took a sharp turn for the worse on Saturday January 28, the pastor lying in a state of semi-consciousness. At 11 o'clock at night, just after his son-in-law had arrived by mail train, he breathed his last.

Herrick's fellow believers were stunned by such a rapid turn of events and could only think of the appropriateness of his sermon the previous Sunday from Isaiah 61:10—'He has covered me with the robe of righteousness.' The sermon had described the hope of Christian believers at the near approach of death. Herrick had chosen this subject following the funeral the day before, being aware how many older people died in the winter months. How well it now seemed to fit his own situation.

Herrick's own funeral took place on the first Saturday in February. Hundreds of his congregation followed the hearse from his home in North Hill along the High Street to the chapel in East Stockwell Street. Many of the shops in the town closed for the day as a mark of respect for such a well-known and loved man of God. The Rev. John Raven of Ipswich preached a memorable sermon, reminding the mourners that only a few days before Herrick had been telling them of the Lamb in the midst of the Throne, who leads his flock by living waters, and wipes all tears from their eyes. Little did he know comparatively of that bliss then: much he knew of it now. And what did they think of that last text their pastor had preached from, concerning the robe of righteousness? Let each of them ask, 'am I dressed in that blessed garment? Where shall I be in eternity if I am without it?'

The preacher then addressed the church members with these words: 'You have lost a dear friend and an honoured father; but, remember that your Father in heaven—the Father of the fatherless—still lives: let your sorrow be turned into joy, and your mourning into praise, that God spared him so long. Let you, his weeping and bereaved church join in the utterance of praise, that for fifty-one years he has gone in and out among you; of late, especially, very seldom absent from his post, bearing you on his heart in the study, and pleading for you in your presence in the pulpit. Like some of you, I have known our departed friend more than thirty years; and the scenes of the year 1836, when that sanctuary was re-opened, are deeply impressed upon my memory, as was the benefit I myself derived—then but a youth in the ministry—from his conversation and from his prayers; and I thank God for my early fellowship with the father now gone to his rest.'

The esteem in which Herrick was held was indicated by other ministers who were present that day: Rev. Dr Seaman, rector of St Andrew's, Greenstead, Rev. W.G. Stedman, a Wesleyan Methodist and close friend of Herrick, Rev. T.W. Davids, the pastor of Lion Walk Congregational church, Colchester, Rev. W.F. Clarkson, and other Dissenting ministers from the locality. On leaving the chapel the procession re-formed, and proceeded through High Street, Queen Street, and St Botolphs Street, to the cemetery, headed by about forty members of the congregation, two abreast, wearing silk hatbands. Some time later, the following words were inscribed on the south face of his tombstone:

Beneath this stone
Waiting for the coming
Of our Lord Jesus Christ
Rest the mortal remains of
The Rev. Joseph Herrick
Who for more than half a century
Was the active and devoted minister
Of the Congregational church
Stockwell Street in this town.
Endowed with superior talents
His highest aim was to consecrate
Them to the service of God.
He was a man of sterling integrity
Who on no consideration would
Deviate from the path of uprightness.
Born March 18, 1794
Died January 28, 1865

The words inscribed on the east face of this monument read:

> This obelisk is erected
> By his three surviving children
> Who feel that the imperishable
> Monument of their father's labors
> Are the names written in Heaven
> Of those led to God
> By his long and faithful ministry.

The tombstone is a 10-foot-high obelisk as pictured opposite.

Figure 13: Herrick's commemorative obelisk

Chapter 14
Appreciating Herrick and learning from his life

Having reached the end of our narration of Herrick's life it is important that we briefly evaluate it. We do not believe that Herrick was some kind of 'stained-glass-window saint.' We recognise he had many faults. We also believe that as a true child of God he went through a period of sharp affliction as a loving Father disciplined him and purified his flawed diamond. This, I believe, is the best way of understanding his experiences when enemies tried to oust him from Stockwell chapel. His life has much to teach Christian and non-Christian alike. He was a man of many gifts, a person who 'wore many hats,' yet chiefly a Bible believing minister whose aim was to glorify God and see sinners won for the kingdom of God. We will attempt to reach an honest conclusion in all the chief areas in which he was active.

Preacher

We are told that Herrick rarely preached from more than scanty notes.[209] A sermon outline on repentance, preserved among family memorabilia, shows much more detail than this comment suggests:

Acts 17:30—'God now commands all men everywhere to repent.'

REPENTANCE

1. Nature of it
2. Need of it

3. Proofs of it
4. All capable of it—all men everywhere

5. Final results of it—Peace—Heaven
• What comfort here for penitent
• Terror for impenitent

Finally:
1. How important that gospel be preached to all
2. Its end only answered when sinners repent
3. Pray for the Spirit of God
4. Repentance is Grace
5. All penitents are saved

If this is typical, it suggests, as the correspondent admits, that his sermons were the results of much thought and study.

This sermon is interesting from a doctrinal point of view. Even though he is a Calvinist, Herrick has no problem in declaring that all men are capable of repentance: God commands all men without distinction to repent, so the call is genuine for all under the sound of it. Later he tells his audience that repentance is a grace—no man is capable of repenting in his own strength, so God must grant it by his prevenient grace; and yet he will do so to all penitents. It is encouraging, from this single example, to see the true scriptural balance of an evangelical Calvinist.

The anonymous newspaper correspondent, who seems to have known Herrick well, gives us a vivid picture of what it was like to listen to his preaching. He continued:[210]

His divisions were accurate—often ingenious; his similes beautiful; his metaphors striking—all easy to be understood; his words fluent, plain, Saxon; his articulation distinct—though not loud, deeply impressive, but with an utter absence of affectation; and, though he might occasionally cause a smile, there was with him no levity; a real sincerity of manner, because sincere himself. His preaching was known and esteemed far beyond Colchester, and beyond the limits of the county; and distinguished men were sometimes seen in his congregations. Wherever he preached he could rivet the attention of the largest assembly by his interesting style, his varied topics, and familiar demonstrations. His usual sermons occupied forty-five minutes; and Sabbath after Sabbath, and at week-day services, might be seen the intellectual and the ignorant, the aged and the young, the wealthy and the poor, all alike looking intently and silently upon that well-known tranquil face. The life itself of the Rev. Joseph Herrick was one of exemplary moral purity; and for a period longer than the medium age of men he continued to proclaim the 'religion of peace,' the 'universal depravity of man,' 'Christ crucified,' 'free redemption for all,' and 'redemption by Christ alone.' What a subject! and what a preacher! His powers of illustrating and impressing Scriptural truths surpassed those of other popular preachers; with a good memory, a well-stored mind, great command of words, and impressive delivery, he was earnest and diligent in his Master's work.

The writer of Herrick's obituary agrees with this evaluation, adding:[211]

In devotion, he greatly excelled. His style of preaching was fluent, plain and impressive, remarkably rich in doctrine and experience, very discriminating and heart-searching. His memory was wonderfully retentive; a storehouse, with a supply for instruction and illustration always ready.

This fund of illustrations only came with much effort on Herrick's part. Although God gave this man a gift for speaking, there can be few preachers who worked as hard as Herrick did to improve that gift. He resolved right at the outset of his ministry to 'be diligent to present himself approved to God, a worker who does not need to be ashamed, rightly dividing the word of truth.' 2 Timothy 3:15. Day after day his diary recorded the study he put in, the 1500 pages of reading a month, not for his own pleasure, but to be more useful as the Lord's servant. The range of literature he became conversant with is truly staggering. He raided most of the sermons from the Puritan period and the 18th century. He became an avid student of Geology—Paley's evidences were very satisfying at the time. He familiarised himself with British, Jewish, Roman and Greek History, showing especial interest in Plutarch's lives. Puritan theology was a favourite of his, and many extracts were read in church meetings. He loved Christian biography, and the lives of famous Christians often crossed his reading desk; he was thrilled and motivated by the lives of great believers such as Col. Gardner, Janeway, Darracott and Whitefield. He spent many months reading Kelly's Geography, so he could get to know the world outside the British Isles and take an intelligent interest in missionary enterprise. His own poetic frame of mind was educated by any poetry he could lay his hands on, though Cowper's Christian works he admired most and quoted in his own writing. He had a special interest in all things related to nature and husbandry and would often be seen chatting knowledgably to local farmers and landowners about cultivation of crops and breeding of cattle. Finally, he kept himself up to date with current church and state affairs by reading Christian magazines and secular writing such as the *Spectator*. With a background such as this, it is not surprising to read of his preaching:[212]

> he was a man of penetrating observation and showed a vast knowledge of man and things. He never departed from the greatest of all truths, but exhibited them prominently with great power and effect.

One of his obituary writers suggests that his public ministrations stretched to 10,900 distinct services. This is equivalent to four services a week for the whole of the 51 years. God certainly gave him a very robust constitution, so much so that he could claim, when illness kept him from preaching in 1860, that he had not been out of the pulpit on the Sabbath for more than 46 years. The fitness God gave him was allied to a determination to preach at all costs, and an overwhelming desire to herald forth the everlasting gospel to all who would listen.

His preaching and teaching were by no means confined to adults. One of his younger congregation, recalling his days in Stockwell chapel nearly 50 years after Herrick's death, had this to say: [213]

> Perhaps the best thing Herrick ever did was his evening 'Talks to the Young' which he preferred to call them to enable him to feel less sermon like and stand amongst the young people on a stool in the table pew, with his clerk— John Rist—beside him. He avoided the sermon form and went through books like 'The Proverbs' and 'The Acts' in consecutive verses, and every Sunday evening was an attraction far outnumbering his own young people.

But what of the fruit of all this preaching? Mere human effort, without the Holy Spirit's enlivening presence, would be labour in vain. Herrick was acutely aware of this, and there are frequent prayers scattered throughout the diary, that God would bless the word to the saving of souls, in spite of the unworthiness of the instrument. God richly blessed his faithful servant. His obituary writer declares:

> He left hundreds of spiritual children to mourn his loss.

The church minute book confirms the effectiveness of

Herrick's spiritual endeavours. When he came to the old Helens Lane Meeting Room in 1814, there were only 4 males and seven aged female members. At the opening of Stockwell Chapel in 1816, there were just 28 members. At his death in 1865, 771 names had been added over the years. A tiny church at the beginning, beset by enemies, had by God's grace grown into a thriving membership of around 275 people. 'Oh, what God has done!' Numbers 23:23.

Pastor and friend

Herrick's relationship with church officers was shaped by his experiences during his early and middle years at Helens Lane. His troubles began during the Unitarian crisis, when the Socinian James Mansfield was his only deacon and drew away like-minded people to act without any reference to him. The harshness with which he was treated then did lasting damage to his nerves and his personality. He became very cautious about working closely in spiritual matters with members of his own church. When he tried to work side by side with his deacons in the difficult 1840s, they rebuffed him and held meetings of their own, even though they had agreed in writing to cooperate with him. In these middle years, he confessed that he had been, 'peculiarly unfortunate in the article of Deacons.' The upshot of this constant rejection was that he became isolated, developed a degree of irritability, and acted in a rather autocratic way within his own church. In an age when most people looked up to 'men of the cloth,' this was not a problem to most of the members, but it was an issue with the church officers.

Herrick had also been let down by fellow ministers during the Unitarian crisis. As we have seen, many of them had tolerated such respectable men as Mansfield and his followers and wondered what all the fuss was about. The only true ministerial supporter at this point was John Thornton, his mentor from Billericay. From personal experience, Thornton was fully aware of the danger of Unitarianism. The Congregational Church in his town had been split asunder by the previous pastor Richard Fry, who had been inducted there in 1781, but had made a non-Trinitarian confession in 1798, and tried to encourage a group of supporters to meet at a separate time in the same church building. The depths to which he had sunk are indicated in the statement he made to the church:[214]

> If you desire Trinitarian worship and to hear that God was reconciled to man by pouring out his wrath upon Christ and that the Salvation of the gospel was purchased literally from his penal Justice, you cannot hear these things from me, so I am decidedly of opinion that they are unscriptural …

Fry had to leave, and John Thornton became the pastor of this church in 1800, the members being definite that they wanted the true, Biblical Trinitarian doctrine taught them. He supported Herrick all along.

Herrick's problems in 1815–1816 sadly isolated him from many of the ministers in the immediate locality of Colchester. It was this isolation that made the problems he experienced in his middle years so acute. The church at Lion Walk was regarded as a rival rather than a friend, and relationships became fraught. Herrick pastored his church on his own, and never attended local, regional or national Congregational gatherings or fraternals where he could have had help and fellowship.

The relationship Herrick had with his congregation and ordinary church members could not be more different from this. At heart, he was a very outgoing, friendly man. Right from the outset he had hundreds of devoted followers who hung on his every word. He was assiduous in the way he visited his members, treating them with great tenderness, bearing them constantly before the Lord in his prayers. Herrick seems to have been happiest with his loyal friend Samuel Blomfield who lived a short distance away and was not a church member. Here he could converse, without any criticism of his church behaviour, as an equal but not a rival.

We cannot hold up Herrick's relationships as a model to be copied. His character had definite flaws, brought about by his very trying circumstances. Through it all, the Lord supported him, forgave him all his trespasses, and deigned to use him for His glory.

Upholder of Gospel Truth

Herrick was unusual in displaying quite extraordinary courage in standing up for the truth against almost overwhelming odds. Has any pastor ever had a more desperate church situation at his induction? A mere handful of members; an influential group of enemies who hated the truth that he loved with all his heart; a legacy of past teaching, antinomian at one end, Unitarian at the other, some of it starting a full sixty years before. Courage came as he prayed—his diary is full of prayers during times of crisis.

Herrick paid a price for upholding Biblical truth: affliction pursued him in the church and in the family too. Yet affliction burned away the dross and purified his faith. One writer said of him after his death:[215]

Regular and reliable in all his actions, there was that gravity and sobriety which was in itself impressive, and yet he was a most cheerful companion; and there are some still thankful in the remembrance that the most tranquil, happy, and intellectual hours of their existence were spent in his society. Folly and deceit of all kinds he held in abhorrence; and it was not with him a question how far distant was the limit to which he might go without being entangled by the customs and allurements of worldly society, nor to what distance he might perhaps safely wander amid questionable pursuits, for no one was more scrupulous than himself to practice all that he commended to others, and to observe that apostolic injunction 'avoid the appearance of evil.'

Perhaps the most appropriate summary of his worth was that written by his friend, the Wesleyan preacher, Rev. W.G. Steadman. The following words, for many years, stood in Stockwell Chapel as a tribute to his memory:[216]

SACRED
TO THE MEMORY OF
THE REVEREND JOSEPH HERRICK
Fifty-one Years
The Beloved and Devoted Pastor
Of this Church and Congregation.
Endowed with Rare Ministerial Qualifications,
He Regaled the Highest Intellect,
While 'The Common People heard Him Gladly.'
His Theme was 'Christ Crucified,'
His Aim, the Salvation of Sinners.
Of His Success, he was Content that
'The Day Shall Declare it.'
His Public Labors ended on the 22nd
and His Life on the 28th of January, 1865,
In the 71st Year of His Age.
'He being Dead yet Speaketh,'
This Tablet is Erected by His Sorrowing People.

May the Lord of the harvest give all true believers the strength to labour on as Bonar's hymn suggests:

Go labour on; spend and be spent,
Thy joy to do the Father's will;
It is the way the Master went;
Should not the servant tread it still?

Go, labour on; 'tis not for naught;
Thy earthly loss is heavenly gain;
Men heed thee, love thee, praise thee not;
The Master praises—what are men?

And if this book is being read by someone who is not a true Christian? What better time than now to flee from your sin, and run to the Saviour of sinners? His arms are open wide to all who will abandon any trust in their own goodness and rely wholly on the blood and righteousness of the Lord Jesus Christ! Remember this:

If you only knew the blessings that Salvation brings
You would never stay away;
If you only saw the table laid with lovely things
You would come to the feast today;
For the Door is open wide, and the Saviour bids you come,
There is nothing you will have to pay!
So be wise and step inside, and do not be like those
Who threw their only chance away!

Appendix 1: A brief summary of heresies taught in the 18th century

Arianism

Arius was an elder in the church in Alexandria and lived ~AD 256–336. His particular error concerned the nature of Jesus Christ. To Arians, Christ is not eternal God, but a created being. They consider Christ to be the highest and greatest of created beings, and misuse Proverbs 8:22–23 'The LORD possessed me at the beginning of His way, Before His works of old. 23: I have been established from everlasting, From the beginning, before there was ever an earth,' to argue their case. The very use of the term everlasting in these verses argues strongly against their conclusions. Herrick's comment in his book Immanuel are: 'No words could set forth more strikingly than these do, the eternity of Christ's existence, and God's delight in him.' The denial of Christ's eternal being obviously demands that Christ cannot be God, the Son co-equal with the Father and Spirit.

The denial of Christ's Deity leads Arians to deny the two undiminished natures of Christ after the incarnation. Rather than being undividedly God and man in one person, they have to assume the pre-incarnate soul of the Christ took on human flesh in the virgin's womb.

Socinianism

Faustus Socinus was an Italian theologian who lived during the time of the Reformation (1539–1604). His final thoughts on Christianity are described in the Racovian Catechism which was published in Poland, the country which imbibed Socinianism first, shortly after Socinus' death. Socinianism extends the errors of Arianism. It is also definitely non-Trinitarian, robbing Christ of his Deity, but it also deprives the death of Christ of any atoning value. Socinians are particularly opposed to the death of Christ being the payment of a debt, or as the satisfaction of God's wrath against sin. This is very consistent on the part of Socinians, because if Christ were a mere man, it is obvious that his death could never atone for his people's sins. The scriptures are clear that the richest of people 'None *of them* can by any means redeem *his* brother, nor give to God a ransom for him ...' Psalm 49:7. But we need only look at one chapter in the Bible to see the falsity of the Socinian position. Isaiah 53 makes it abundantly clear:

Isaiah 53:5 But He was wounded for our transgressions, He was bruised for our iniquities; the chastisement for our peace was upon Him, and by His stripes we are healed.

Isaiah 53:10 Yet it pleased the LORD to bruise Him; He has put Him to grief. When You make His soul an offering for sin, He shall see His seed, He shall prolong His days, and the pleasure of the LORD shall prosper in His hand.

The fear of the Socinians, and all those who wanted a rational religion, was that 'free grace' would lead to a loss of piety: people would have no incentive to live a holy life. This very issue is of course thoroughly dealt with in the scriptures: 'shall we continue in sin that grace may abound? Certainly not! Etc.' Romans 6:1. The Socinian religion in the end becomes a dead religion of good works, completely devoid of God's grace; it becomes a hollow and negative religion, noted more for what it does not believe than for what it does.

The term Socinian was very much disliked by those who believed its tenets. It became a term of abuse, a description of a heretic. Socinians claimed to be descendants of the earliest English Presbyterians, who were godly Trinitarians, and shamelessly occupied the church buildings which once rung with the doctrine of the cross. It became a proverb among Dissenters that 'Socinianism, with cuckoo insidiousness takes possession of nests she never built, and hatches her brood in stolen habitations.' The dislike many felt at this behaviour led eventually to the change of name to Unitarian by a new group of people who were not descendants of the original English Presbyterians and felt free to modify Socinian beliefs and add further heterodox doctrines.

Unitarianism

We have no need to repeat here what was said in Chapter 3 about the lack of meaning in this new term. Unitarianism in its new format was the brainchild of Theophilus Lindsey and Joseph Priestley in the 1770s. By the time Herrick was in Colchester, Unitarianism was no longer prohibited by law, and soon after it had both its own Bible translation and Unitarian publications. Unitarianism is better defined by what it does not believe, rather than what it does. In the 1810s, it still purported to be scripturally based, much as today the Christadelphians and Jehovah's Witnesses make the same claim. Unitarianism, however, has no fixed beliefs; this was always the case with the descendants of English Presbyterians who believed that human reason must be the final arbiter of truth. Unitarianism was on a journey into unbelief; it still is. Setting out by accepting Socinian beliefs concerning the person and work of Christ, it soon went about altering Scripture to agree with its errors. When James Martineau (1805–1900) became very influential among them, Scripture itself was abandoned as the ground of truth. The Unitarians have changed again during the 20th and 21st centuries. They are now a multi-faith organisation, accepting there are many paths to God.

It is instructive to list the more famous people who have been linked in some way, or strongly influenced by or influential in the spread of Unitarianism:

Robert Burns (1759–1796), Scottish poet.

Henry Cavendish (1731–1810), Cambridge Chemist—note Cavendish Laboratories in Cambridge.

Samuel Clarke (1675–1729), tutored Philip Doddridge and was censored by Cambridge and the Church of England for his writings on the Trinity.

Chamberlain family in Birmingham—Austin, Joseph and Neville; the latter Prime Minister before Churchill.

Samuel Taylor Coleridge (1772–1834), English poet, educated in a Unitarian school in Shrewsbury.

Courtauld family, famous synthetic fibre industrialists.

Charles Darwin (1809–1882), Propounder of the theory of evolution. Born and educated in Shrewsbury, his mother was a Wedgwood and a Unitarian. Charles went to a school whose headmaster was a Unitarian. The Shrewsbury Unitarian Church tells us that Charles Darwin worshipped in that church when he was young.

Charles Dickens (1812–1870), novelist.

Elizabeth Gaskell (1810–1865), novelist.

Sir Charles Lyell (1797–1875), uniformitarian geologist.

John Milton (1608–1674), poet.

Frances William Newman (1805–1897), brother of John Henry

Newman. FW was in the Plymouth Brethren in the early days, but drifted into Unitarianism.

Sir Isaac Newton (1642–1726), famous physicist.

Florence Nightingale (1820–1910), philanthropist of Crimean war. Her grandfather on her mother's side was William Smith, the Unitarian MP, responsible for bringing in the Doctrine of the Trinity Act of 1813, which allowed Unitarians to worship legally.

Beatrix Potter (1866–1943), children's author. Both her parents were Manchester Unitarians.

Robert Robinson (1735–1790), hymn writer—'Come thou fount of every blessing.' Started as a Baptist, 'converted' through Whitefield. Came under influence of Joseph Priestley and preached in Unitarian church in Cambridge; died in Birmingham; funeral conducted by Priestley. A sad case.

Albert Schweitzer (1875–1965), theologian and friend of Unitarians.

Sir Henry Tate (1819–1899), sugar magnate and art donor.

Wedgwood family.

With such a list it is clear that they have influenced the thinking of millions of people.

It is staggering now, to think that in the 1810s when the Unitarians were flexing their muscles, so many Dissenters accepted them as fellow Christians and fellow Dissenters. There are lessons for today, surely.

Appendix 2: A selection of Herrick's hymns from his own hymn book

Herrick's hymnbook can be seen in Dr Williams's library in London. Its title is:

A selection of evangelical hymns: doctrinal, practical, and experimental, compiled by J. Herrick—Third edition, enlarged. Publisher: Colchester: published by S.F. Fenton; sold also by Longman and Co. and Hamilton and Co, London 1836. 284p, 12cm.

No 8   LM

1. This sacred day, great Lord is thine,
And here at thy command we meet,
O may we see thy glory shine,
While looking to thy mercy-seat!

2. With joy we saw the morning light
Of a new day of holy rest;
A day in which the saints delight
And of all days esteem the best.

3. While strangers to thy heavenly grace
Pursue their sins, profane thy day,
We hither haste to seek thy face,
To hear thy word, and praise and pray.

4. Lord, while we come before thy throne,
Our minds compose, warm every heart;
And sinful thoughts and cares be gone,
And make our doubts and fears depart.

5. Let worship raise our souls from earth,
And teach us to commune with heaven;
May many learn a Saviour's worth,
And fly to him to be forgiven.

6. Eternal Spirit! Now descend,
With thy rich influence fill the place;
That we with profit may attend
The instituted means of grace.

No 9   8 7 8 7 8 7

1. Come poor sinners, Christ invites you,
Quickly, then, to him apply.
He, alone, your sins can pardon,
He, alone your wants supply:
Do not linger!
You must come to him or die!

2. Though your sins are great and many,
That will no objection prove,
We have all in sin abounded,
But our Lord abounds in love:
Fall before him!
You will his compassion move!

3. Even now he looks towards you,
Mercy beaming from his eye;
Waiting only to be gracious,
Soon as you for mercy cry:
He will never
Leave a penitent to die!

4. Let not unbelief or Satan
Keep you from the Saviour's throne;
Your concern for his salvation
Proves that light has on you shone:
Nature cannot
Make our need of Jesus known.

5. Come then, with your guilt and sorrow,
To a Saviour full of grace;
He invites you—he will pardon
Sons of Adam's ruined race:
If you seek him,
You with joy, shall see his face.

No 10 SM

1. Our hearts, by nature, Lord,
Are hardened and impure,
Insensible beneath thy word,
Against alarm secure.

2. The preacher's close appeal
Can no impression make;
Nor awful death, nor thoughts of hell
Their stubborn firmness shake.

3. Sin ready entrance meets
In every loathsome form;
But Jesus, though he long intreats,
Scarce enters but by storm.

4. Great Lord! The cause is thine;
Thy Spirit's power impart,
Here as a mighty Conqueror shine,
And vanquish every heart.

5. Enter with all thy train,
Faith hope and holy love;
Be sin expelled—break every chain,
That we may rise above.

No 54 7 7 7 7

1. If the Saviour's name we bear,
We should live by faith and prayer;
Zealous of his glory be;
And from sinful practice free.

2. If we any sin allow,
Or neglect the 'throne of grace,'
Faith and hope will soon be low,
Jesus soon will hide his face.

3. And the sun's warm influence gone,
Holy love will fast decay,
Soon the heart grow hard as stone,
Graces freeze, and die away.

4. Gracious Lord! Be ever near;
Leave us not we humbly pray,
All our poor petitions hear,
Keep us that we may not stray.

5. In thy cause may we be bold,
Strong in faith, and warm with love;
Never lukewarm, never cold,
Never Lord, thy absence prove.

No 61 LM

1. Stay, stay, thou thoughtless sinner, stay,
Oh! Hear what Jesus has to say:—
'Soon shall my awful throne arise
Upon the clouds in yonder skies.'

2. And canst thou all the terrors brave,
Of sickness, pain, death, and the grave;
With all the thoughts that crowd the mind
Of future pains, or joys refined?

3. Oh! Listen to the gospel's voice,
And make its holy ways thy choice;
Then time may quickly onward roll,
Nor yet the thought dismay thy soul.

4. Days, months and years may haste away,
And nearer bring the final day;
But grace the new born spirit buoys,
And seals the hope of endless joys.

5. Great God! Thy blessing now impart,
Oh! Send thy word to every heart;
Let thoughtless minds be serious made,
And all be more of sin afraid.

No 78 7 7 7 7

1. Thoughtless sinner! Come and see
Jesus hung on Calvary;
See him languish! Hear him groan!
Know, for men he left his throne.

2. See! His head a crown adorns,
Not of gold—a crown of thorns!
See the blood that o'er him flows!
'Tis a balm for all thy woes.

3. See his pierced hands and feet;
And his heart with love replete;
See him bow his languid head!
See him now among the dead!

4. Hast thou never thought before?
Think then, now, what Jesus bore;
Think of Jesus crucified;
Know for sin he bled and died.

5. 'Twas thy sin caused every smart;
Pierced his hand, and feet and heart;
Made him intimate with grief,
Made him die for thy relief.

6. Come, poor sinner, to thy Friend;
He will all thy wants attend:
Those who for his mercy cry,
He will never leave to die.

Bibliography

1. S.W. Amos, *Social discontent and Agrarian disturbances in Essex, 1795–1850* (Durham theses, Durham University, 1971). Available at Durham E-Theses Online.

2. Charles Benham, *Colchester worthies. A biographical index of Colchester* (London and Colchester, 1892). Available on line.

3. James Bennett, *The history of Dissenters, during the last thirty years, (from 1808 to 1838)* (1839). Available on line.

4. Blomfields, *The Blomfields of Dedham and Colchester* (Published privately by L.C. Sier, 1924). Available in Colchester Borough Library.

5. A.F.J. Brown, *Essex People 1750–1900, from their diaries, memoirs and letters* (Published by Essex County Council, Chelmsford. Essex Record Office Publication No.59, 1972). Information from a few people who lived in Herrick's time, and interacted with him.

6. C. Gordon Bolam, Jeremy Goring, H.L. Short and Roger Thomas, *The English Presbyterians. From Elizabethan Puritanism to Modern Unitarianism* (London: George Allen & Unwin, 1968). A very useful history of the Presbyterian denomination from the earliest time, showing how they drifted more and more into heterodox belief.

7. *Book No. 6 Lion Walk Church*. The most significant church minute book for the period when both Lion Walk and Stockwell Chapels were flourishing. Available from Essex Record Office as D/NC 52/2/1.

8. Charles Buck, *Memoirs and remains of the late Rev. Charles Buck*, John Styles, London, printed for Hamilton, Adams, and

Co., 1817. Available on line.

9. J. Hay Colligan, *The Arian movement in England* (Manchester University Press, 1913). Available on line.

10. *Congregationalists in Crisis 1836–1843* (Colchester local Historical Society, Colchester Borough Library). An excellent analysis of the events surrounding the attempt to force Herrick from Stockwell Chapel in the period from 1839 to 1843. Available at Colchester Borough Library.

11. Thomas W. Davids, *Annals of Evangelical Nonconformity in the county of Essex, from the time of Wycliffe to the restoration, with memorials of the Essex ministers who were silenced, and brief notices of the Essex churches which originated with their labours* (London: Jackson Walford and Hodder, 1863).

12. Alan C. Clifford, *Philip Doddridge, The Good doctor, Philip Doddridge of Northampton, a tercentenary tribute* (Norwich: Charenton Reformed Publishing, 2002).

13. J.D. Humphreys (ed.), *The correspondence and diary of Philip Doddridge* (1829). Available on line.

14. Thomas Steadman (ed.), *Letters to and from the Rev. Philip Doddridge D.D.* (1790). Available on line.

15. Josiah Gilbert (ed.), *Autobiography and other memorials of Mrs Ann Gilbert* (3rd Edition, London: 1878). Very useful for church background in Colchester in the last years of the 18th century. Available on line.

16. Alfred Goodall, 'Early Independency in Essex', *Transactions Congregational Historical Society*, Vol VI, No 3, February 1914. Available on line.

17. *Helens Lane Old Church Minute Book, 1796 to 1816.*

Strangely, still in the possession of the Herrick family. Covers the whole of Isaac Taylor's, Joseph Drake's and Joseph Herrick's ministry until the unroofing of the chapel in June 1816. Available as a transcribed Microsoft Word document from the author on request.

18. Joseph Herrick, *Commonplace Book and Journal*, 1813. (Denoted *Diary* in the text.) It covers the period from 29 September 1813 till 14 April 1819, with the whole of 1858 as a separate document inside. Unpublished, family owned document. Available as a transcribed Microsoft Word document from the author on request.

19. Joseph Herrick, *Poetic and Prosaic Sketches*. Written from 1812 onwards, in the possession of the Herrick family. Unpublished, but also available as a transcribed Microsoft Word document from the author on request.

20. Joseph Herrick, *Immanuel; being a collection of scriptures, relating to the person and work of the Lord Jesus Christ with cursory remarks in twenty-five letters to a friend, designed to show that the Bible is against Socinians* (Chelmsford: I. Marsden, 1819). Referred to simply as *Immanuel*. Copy still available in Colchester borough library.

21. Joseph Herrick, *The Monitory Mirror: exhibiting the marks, causes and consequences of indifference in religion, and also the means of restoration to consistency* (London: The Religious Tract Society, 1836). Available on line.

22. Joseph Herrick, *The greatness of God's mercy in Christ, or salvation possible to the vilest sinners* (London: Simpkin, Marshall and Co, 1842). Available on line.

23. Joseph Herrick, *Salvation certain and complete, or the greatest sinners capable of being rendered holy and happy* (London: Simpkin, Marshall and Co, 1845). Available on line.

24. *Congregational Year Book*, 1866, obituary of Joseph Herrick.

25. Joseph Herrick, *Stockwell Chapel Minute Book, 1816–1865*. Available at Essex Record Office, Chelmsford under code D/NC 42/1/1. Available also as a transcribed Microsoft Word document from the author on request.

26. Joseph Herrick, 'A Brief historical sketch of the Church of Christ Meeting in Helens Lane, Colchester'. Original written in March 1821, reproduced in *Transactions Congregational Historical Society*, Vol. VII, No 4, October 1917. Available on line.

27. Janet Cooper and C.R. Elrington (eds.), *History of the County of Essex*: Volume 9, the Borough of Colchester, (London: Victoria County History, 1994). Gives excellent summary of all the Dissenting churches in Colchester for the period of interest. Available on line.

28. John Hyatt, *A discourse delivered at Ebenezer Chapel, Shadwell, February 19, 1826, on the occasion of the death of the Reverend John Hyatt, containing a full account of his early life, by Charles Hyatt* (London: 1826). Available on line.

29. James Mansfield, *Priestly Tyranny Exposed*. A short statement of the causes of the disunion and division which took place in the congregation assembling in Helen's Lane, Colchester, in which the conduct of the Rev. Joseph Herrick is set in its true light (Colchester: U.W. Mattacks, and London: D. Eaton, 1817). A scurrilous attack on the character of Herrick by the Unitarian trustee James Mansfield who led the opposition to Herrick and organised the unroofing of the chapel in June 1816. Copy available in the library of Essex University at Colchester.

30. Stephen Owen, 'Whatever happened at Salters Hall?' Three

articles in *Evangelical Times*, August, September and October 2016

31. Irene Parker, *Dissenting academies in England, their rise and progress, and their place among the educational systems of the country* (Cambridge University Press, 1914).

32. Andrew Phillips, *Colchester, A History* (Phillimore & Co, 2004). A useful history of Colchester by a local historian in the city.

33. Herbert S. Skeats, *A history of the Free Churches of England: from AD 1688–AD 1851* (1869). Available on line.

34. James A. Tabor, A brief history of the Independent Church assembling in the Lion Walk, Colchester, from 1641 to 1861, Colchester, 1861.

35. Jane Taylor, *The writings of Jane Taylor* in three volumes, Volume 1 (Boston: 1835). Available on line.

36. Peter Toon, *The emergence of Hyper-Calvinism in English Nonconformity, 1689–1765* (London: The Olive Tree, 1967).

37. Francis Westley, *The Manchester Socinian Controversy*; with introductory remarks and an appendix, C. Westley and Tyrrell (Dublin, 1825). The opening debate on the legitimacy of Socinian/Unitarian worshippers occupying church buildings originally built for orthodox Christians. This began in Manchester and a few cases of 'illegal occupancy' were tried before Chancery courts. Such cases were closed in 1844 by the Dissenters Chapels Act, which prevented hundreds of such cases being decided upon. Occupancy of 25 years or more was deemed sufficient to prove legitimate occupancy by a heterodox denomination. Available on line.

38. Arnold A. Dallimore, *George Whitefield: The life and times of the great evangelist of the 18th century revival* (London: The Banner of Truth Trust, 1970).

39. Joshua Wilson, *Memoir of the Life and Character of Thomas Wilson Esq, by his son* (London: 1849). Available on line.

Endnotes

Abbreviations

HLMB   *Helens Lane Meeting Room Minute Book, 1796 - 1816*

SMB   *Stockwell Church Minute Book, 1816 - 1865*

Chapter 1

1. Brief Historical Sketch of the Church of Christ Meeting in Helens Lane, Colchester' by Joseph Herrick, *Transactions Congregational Historical Society*, Vol VII, No 4, October 1917, p. 254.
2. Opening page of *SMB*, 'Origin of St. Helens Lane Congregational Church, Colchester.'
3. Obituary, *Congregational Year Book*, 1866.

Chapter 2

4. Death of the Rev. Joseph Herrick, *Essex Standard*, Wednesday 1 February 1865.
5. As seen in: http://www.wolverhamptonhistory.org.uk/work/industry/steel_jewellery, accessed January 2017.
6. Images courtesy of Wolverhampton Arts and Culture.
7. Verses 166–7, 'The Domestic Christian', from *Poetic and Prosaic Sketches*, Herrick.
8. Verse 169, 'The Domestic Christian', from *Poetic and Prosaic Sketches*, Herrick.
9. A history of Wolverhampton written in 1985 to celebrate the town's millennium by the late Keith Farley: *Wolverhampton 985–1985 with special reference to Frank Mason and Geoff Pennock*. http://www.historywebsite.co.uk/history/farley/oldwlv.htm, accessed 28/03/2016.
10. Verse 175, 'The Domestic Christian', from Joseph Herrick, *Poetic and Prosaic Sketches*.
11. Verses 179–180, 'The Domestic Christian', from Joseph Herrick, *Poetic and Prosaic*

Sketches.

12. August 6, 1862, *SMB.*

13. Chapter 7, 'The Great Change—Conversion', in C.H. Spurgeon *Autobiography*, Volume 1: The Early Years, 1834–1859 (London: The Banner of Truth Trust, 1962).

14. Lady Huntingdon—Selina Hastings (1707–1791)—was a rich Christian lady who was a great supporter of the Methodist revival and gave money for chapels to be built in numerous parts of the country. Churches which still exist are described as Lady Huntingdon's Connexion.

15. Verses 186 and 191, 'The Domestic Christian', from Joseph Herrick, *Poetic and Prosaic Sketches.*

16. Obituary, *Congregational Year Book* 1866.

17. Hymn No 3 in 'A selection of evangelical hymns: doctrinal, practical, and experimental,' compiled by J. Herrick, Third edition, enlarged, Published, Colchester: publisher, S.F. Fenton; sold by Longman and Co, Hamilton and Co, London 1836. Dr Williams's Library, London.

18. *Memoirs and remains of the late Rev. Charles Buck* (John Styles, London, printed for Hamilton, Adams, and Co., 1817).

19. Dissenting Academies OnLine: http://dissacad.english.qmul.ac.uk/ accessed 29/3/2016.

20. 'On Entering the Ministry,' in Joseph Herrick, *Poetic and Prosaic Sketches.*

21. Joseph Herrick's will, 1827.

Chapter 3

22. C. Gordon Bolam, Jeremy Goring, H.L. Short, Roger Thomas, *The English Presbyterians* (London: George Allen & Unwin Ltd, 1968), p. 54.

23. *Reliquiae Baxterianae*: Mr Baxter's narrative of the most memorable passages of his life and times, ed. Matthew Sylvester, Book iii, 1696, p. 67.

24. Arnold A. Dallimore, *George Whitefield: The life and times of the great evangelist of the 18th century revival* (London: The Banner of Truth Trust, 1970), p. 25.

25. Quoted in *Letters to and from Dr Doddridge*, p. 51, in Walter Wilson, *The History and Antiquities of Dissenting Churches and Meeting Houses in London, Westminster and Southwark*, 4 volumes, Volume 2 (London: Walter Wilson, 1808), p. 96.

26. Peter Toon, *The emergence of Hyper-Calvinism in English Nonconformity, 1689–1765*

(London: The Olive Tree, 1967), p. 33.

27. John Locke, *The Reasonableness of Christianity*, p. 95–96, downloaded from www.fedaralistpapers.org, early 2017.

28. Richard Baxter, *The Saints Everlasting Rest*, pt 2, 5.

29. C. Gordon Bolam, Jeremy Goring, H.L. Short, Roger Thomas, *The English Presbyterians* (London: George Allen & Unwin Ltd, 1968) pp. 155–156.

30. Unitarian was a term used from the late 18th century to describe someone who believed that only God the Father is God. Not only did it deny the deity of Jesus Christ and the Holy Spirit, it also denied the atoning, propitiatory death of Christ. The term was popularised by Joseph Priestley the ardent proponent of Unitarianism. See Appendix 1 for a fuller treatment.

31. C. Gordon Bolam, Jeremy Goring, H.L. Short, Roger Thomas, *The English Presbyterians* (London: George Allen & Unwin Ltd, 1968), pp. 169–170.

32. C. Gordon Bolam, Jeremy Goring, H.L. Short, Roger Thomas, *The English Presbyterians* (London: George Allen & Unwin Ltd, 1968), p. 161.

33. 'Congregationalists and the Great Ejectment', *Transactions Congregational Historical Society*, VI, No 1, February 1913, pp. 25–34.

34. Taking the total number of ejected ministers as being roughly 2,000.

35. James Bennett, DD, *History of the Dissenters during the last 30 years, (from 1808 to 1838)* (London: 1839), pp. 264–265, data corrected from tables.

36. Herbert S. Skeats and Charles S. Miall, *History of the Free Churches of England 1688–1891*, p. 265.

37. Of Watts' deviations, Toplady writes in pages 121–132, *Works*, Volume 14, 'Outlines of the life of Dr Watts': 'Gladly would I throw, if possible, an everlasting veil over this valuable person's occasional deviations from the simplicity of the gospel, relative to the personality and divinity of the Son and Spirit of God. But justice compels me to acknowledge that he did not always preserve an uniform consistency with himself, nor with the scriptures of truth, so far as concerns that grand and fundamental article of the Christian faith. The inconclusiveness (to call it by the tenderest name we can) of his too wanton tamperings with the doctrine of the Trinity, has been largely and irrefragably demonstrated by more hands than one.'

38. See pp. 382–384 of Doddridge's 'A course of lectures on the principle subjects in pneumatology, ethics and divinity with references to the most considerable authors on each subject,' by the late Rev. Philip Doddridge, the second edition corrected (London: 1776).

39. See Appendix 1 for more details.

40. Letter to Samuel Clarke, Sept 1722, in John Doddridge Humphreys (ed.), *The Correspondence and Diary of Philip Doddridge* (1829), pp. 155–156.

41. Alan C. Clifford, *The Good Doctor, Philip Doddridge of Northampton—A Tercentenary Tribute* (Norwich: Charenton Reformed Publishing, 2002), p. 90,

42. http://dissacad.english.qmul.uk/ Accessed January 2017.

43. http://dissacad.english.qmul.uk/ Accessed January 2017.

44. http://dissacad.english.qmul.ac.uk/sample1.php?detail=achist&histid=74&acadid=42#tabs-2, accessed 12/01/2017.

45. John Towill Rutt (ed.), *Life and correspondence of Joseph Priestley LLD, FRS etc.*, Vol. 1 (London: 1831), footnote p. 5.

46. Preface to Joseph Herrick, *Immanuel* (London, Ipswich and Colchester: 1819).

47. Herbert S. Skeats and Charles S. Miall, *History of the Free Churches of England 1688–1891*, p.306.

48. D. Bogue and J. Bennett, *History of Dissenters from the Revolution in 1688 to the year 1806*, Volume 4 (1812), p. 313.

Chapter 4

49. *The Nonconformist Memorial*, originally written by Edmund Calamy, abridged etc., by Samuel Palmer, 2nd Edition, Vol 2, 1802, p. 191.

50. *The Nonconformist Memorial*, originally written by Edmund Calamy, abridged etc., by Samuel Palmer, 2nd Edition, Vol 2 (1802), p 195.

51. 'Brief Historical Sketch of the Church of Christ Meeting in Helens Lane, Colchester', by Joseph Herrick, *Transactions Congregational Historical Society*, Vol VII, No 4, October 1917, p. 256.

52. 'Brief Historical Sketch of the Church of Christ Meeting in Helens Lane, Colchester', by Joseph Herrick, *Transactions Congregational Historical Society*, Vol VII, No 4, October 1917, p. 256.

53. John Tren, 'Persecution displayed,' in a sermon preached at Colchester, to a congregation of Protestant Dissenters on November 5, 1732, pp. 15–18.

54. Jerom Murch, minister of Trim Street chapel, Bath, *History of the Presbyterian and General Baptist churches in the west of England; with memoirs of some of their pastors*

(London: 1835), pp. 201–203 etc.

55. *The posthumous works of the late learned and reverend Isaac Watts*, Vol 2, (Doddridge to Watts April 23, 1740), p. 43.

56. Alfred Goodall, 'Early Independency in Essex,' *Transactions Congregational Historical Society*, Vol VI, No 3, February 1914, p. 156.

57. 'Brief Historical Sketch of the Church of Christ Meeting in Helens Lane, Colchester, by Joseph Herrick', *Transactions Congregational Historical Society*, Vol VII, No 4, October 1917, p. 257.

58. 'Brief Historical Sketch of the Church of Christ Meeting in Helens Lane, Colchester, by Joseph Herrick', *Transactions Congregational Historical Society*, Vol VII, No 4, October 1917, pp. 257–8.

59. Early Independency in Essex, by Alfred Goodall, *Transactions Congregational Historical Society*, Vol VI, No 3, February 1914, p 157.

60. Josiah Gilbert (ed.), *Autobiography and other memorials of Mrs Gilbert* (3rd Edition, London: 1878), pp. 62–63.

61. Much of this section generally from *HLMB*.

62. March 1, 1799, *HLMB*.

63. May 27, 1808, *HLMB*.

64. Josiah Gilbert (ed.), *Autobiography and other memorials of Mrs Gilbert* (3rd Edition, London: 1878), pp.70–71.

65. This was almost certainly William Kemp, copastor when Giles Hobbs was infirm. He was never ordained at Lion Walk; his sermons were not designed to be popular!

66. Josiah Gilbert (ed.), *Autobiography and other memorials of Mrs Gilbert* (3rd Edition, London: 1878), p. 130.

67. Josiah Gilbert (ed.), *Autobiography and other memorials of Mrs Gilbert* (3rd Edition, London: 1878), p. 131.

68. *The writings of Jane Taylor in three volumes*, Volume 1, Boston, 1835), p. 34.

69. Josiah Gilbert (ed.), *Autobiography and other memorials of Mrs Gilbert* (3rd Edition, London: 1878), p. 137, footnote.

70. *The Congregational Magazine*, April 1835, p. 264.

71. *The Congregational Magazine*, April 1835, p. 264.

72. 'Brief Historical Sketch of the Church of Christ Meeting in Helens Lane, Colchester, by Joseph Herrick, *Transactions Congregational Historical Society*, Vol VII, No 4, October 1917, p. 258.

73. Scrapbooks assembled during late 19th century by Alderman John Bawtree Harvey of Colchester, (1809–1890), Essex Record Office, C210 Box 7.

74. Usually spelled Ignis Fatuus, meaning a 'will o' the wisp.'

75. March 1, 1812, *HLMB*.

Chapter 5

76. January 1814, *HLMB*.

77. Reproduced by courtesy of Essex Record Office, reference, 1/Pb 8/16/2.

78. Verses 209–210, 'The Domestic Christian,' in Joseph Herrick, *Poetic and Prosaic Sketches*.

79. May 15, 1804, *HLMB*.

80. Josiah Gilbert (ed.), *Autobiography and other memorials of Mrs Gilbert* (3rd Edition, London: 1878), p. 68.

Chapter 6

81. Sunday March 19, 1815, *HLMB*.

82. March 31, 1815, *HLMB*.

83. April 10, 1815, *HLMB*.

84. J. Mansfield, *Priestly tyranny exposed etc.* (U.W. Mattacks, Colchester and D. Eaton, London, 1817), p. 12.

85. December 6, 1816, *SMB*.

86. Preface, Joseph Herrick, *Immanuel* (1819).

87. May 5, 1815, *HLMB*.

88. June 14, 1815, *HLMB*.

89. J. Mansfield, *Priestly tyranny exposed etc.*, (U.W. Mattacks, Colchester and D. Eaton, London, 1817), pp. 14–15.

90. J. Mansfield, *Priestly tyranny exposed etc.*, (U.W. Mattacks, Colchester and D. Eaton, London, 1817), p. 22.

91. J. Mansfield, *Priestly tyranny exposed etc.*, (U.W. Mattacks, Colchester and D. Eaton, London, 1817), pp. 26–27.

92. http://booty.org.uk/booty.weather/climate/histclimat.htm. Accessed 14/03/2017.

93. Nicholas Klingaman, Floods, Famine, Frosts and Frankenstein in 'The Year Without Summer' in http://www.huffingtonpost.com/nicholas-klingaman/the-year-without-summer_b_2877422.html, accessed 21/03/2017.

94. S.W. Amos, (1971) *Social discontent and Agrarian disturbances in Essex, 1795–1850*, pp. 31–32. Durham theses, Durham University. Available at Durham E-Theses Online: http://etheses.dur.ac.uk/10399/.

95. https://www.poetryfoundation.org/poems/43825/darkness-56d222aeeee1b, accessed 12/02/2017.

96. '1816, the year without a summer,' Radio 4 broadcast 'In Our Time,' Melvyn Bragg and guests, 21/04/2016.

97. Andrew Phillips, *Colchester, A History* (Phillimore, 2004), p. 69.

98. S.W. Amos (1971) *Social discontent and Agrarian disturbances in Essex, 1795–1850*, Durham theses, Durham University, p. 3, Available at Durham E-Theses Online: http://etheses.dur.ac.uk/10399/.

99. *Georgian Colchester Economic History*, http://www.british-history.ac.uk/vch/essex/vol9/pp135-147#h3-0002 accessed 14/03/2017.

100. J. Mansfield, *Priestly tyranny exposed etc*. (U.W. Mattacks, Colchester and D. Eaton, London, 1817), p. 6.

101. 'A series of letters addressed to the church and congregation assembling at the Great Meeting, Coggeshall, containing a complete narrative, of the cruel and unmerited persecution of which the Rev. J. Fielding has been the subject for more than twelve months past. Written by himself' (1815). 210 pages, AND, 'A rejoinder to the letters addressed to the church and congregation assembling at the Great Meeting House, Coggeshall, together with some remarks on the reply and vindication recently published. By the Rev. J. Fielding' (1816), 97 pages.

102. 'A reply to the recently published letters of the Rev. J. Fielding to the church assembling at the Great Meeting Room, Coggeshall, and a vindication of the persons aspersed in those' (Colchester, Printed T. Marsden, 34 Culver Street, circa 1816). 65 pages.

Chapter 7

103. Opening pages, *SMB*.

104. 'A Brief historical sketch of the Church of Christ Meeting in Helens Lane, Colchester.

Original written by Joseph Herrick in March 1821', reproduced in *Transactions Congregational Historical Society* Vol VII, No 4, October 1917, p. 260.

105. September 7, 1824, *SMB.*

106. Letter Joseph Herrick to Thomas Wilson, April 30, 1834: Dr Williams's Library, London.

107. May 30, 1834, *SMB.*

108. Letter to T. Wilson Esq, February 10, 1835; Dr Williams's Library, London.

109. October 4,1836, *SMB.*

110. P724, the *Congregational Magazine*, November 1836.

111. March 31, 1826, *SMB.*

112. October 6, 1832, *SMB.*

113. March 30, 1838, *SMB.*

114. Courtesy of Tina Salmon, photographed 11/08/2016, then transcribed.

Chapter 9

115. James Bennett DD, *History of Dissenters in the last 30 years, (from 1808 to 1838)* (London: 1839) p. 358.

116. CENSUS, 1801–1981; COLCHESTER BOROUGH COUNCIL, COLCHESTER COUNTS (Mar. 1993), 13.

117. Book No. 6 Lion Walk Church, Essex Record Office, D/NC 52/2/1, p. 54.

118. December 2, 1836, *SMB.*

119. August 5, 1832, *SMB.*

120. *Essex Standard*, Wednesday 1 February 1865, Death of the Rev. Joseph Herrick.

121. *A History of the County of Essex*, Volume 9, the Borough of Colchester, http://www.british-history.ac.uk/vch/essex/vol9. Originally published by Victoria County History, (London: 1994), pp. 339–351.

122. *Essex Standard*, 8 Mar. 1839.

123. Book No. 6 Lion Walk Church, Essex Record Office, D/NC 52/2/1, p. 117.

124. 'A brief history of the Independent Church assembling in the Lion Walk, Colchester, from 1641 to 1861', James A. Tabor (Colchester: 1861), p. 57.

125. 'The substance of a statement laid before the members of the church of Christ assembling in the Lion Walk, Colchester, on Monday evening, February 3, 1845, by T.W. Davids, pastor', p. 9.

126. *Essex Standard*, Friday 20 February 1846.

127. *Essex Standard*, Friday 22 March 1844.

128. *Essex Standard*, Wednesday 21 May 1862.

129. *Memoir of the Life and Character of Thomas Wilson Esq.*, by his son (London: John Snow, 1849), p. 195–196.

130. A.F.J. Brown, *Essex people 1750–1900, from their diaries and letters* (Essex County Council, Chelmsford, 1972), p. 121.

Chapter 10

131. An excellent analysis of the events in this chapter can be read in *Congregationalists in Crisis 1836–1843* (Colchester local Historical Society, Colchester Borough Library).

132. Andrew Phillips, *Colchester, A History* (2004), p. 99.

133. Book No. 6 Lion Walk Church, Essex Record Office, D/NC 52/2/1, p. 97.

134. Book No. 6 Lion Walk Church, Essex Record Office, D/NC 52/2/1, p. 96.

135. Book No. 6 Lion Walk Church, Essex Record Office, D/NC 52/2/1, p. 104.

136. February 10, 1835, Letter from Joseph Herrick to Thomas Wilson, Dr Williams's Library, London.

137. A fifth column is any group of people who undermine a larger group from within, usually in favour of an enemy group or nation. The activities of a fifth column can be overt or clandestine. Wikipedia: https://en.wikipedia.org/wiki/Fifth_column, accessed 20/04/2017.

138. 'Tale of two chapels', *Essex County Standard*, 4 July 1991, local history with Andrew Phillips.

139. The letter is preserved amongst the collection of material amassed by J.B. Harvey and preserved in Colchester Borough Library: it is to be found in the small brown book, pp. 119–120.

140. 'Tale of two chapels', *Essex County Standard*, 4 July 1991, local history with Andrew Phillips.

141. Reproduced by courtesy of the Essex Record Office, reference, C210 Box 7.

142. Scrapbook assembled during late 19th century by Alderman John Bawtree Harvey of Colchester, (1809–1890), Essex Record Office, C210 Box 7.

143. Andrew Phillips, *Colchester, A History* (Phillimore and Co., 2004), p. 98.

144. Courtesy, Tina Salmon, photographed 11/08/2016, then transcribed.

145. April 4, 1829, *SMB*.

146. April 2, 1839, *SMB*.

147. Immediately after Savill's resignation, only the male members appear to have met, and agreed by 30 votes to one to ask him to return as co-pastor with Henry March. (This is far too small a number to be the whole membership, male and female). When Savill agreed to their terms, they then invited March to take the co-pastorship, and the minute book tells us, revealingly: it was unanimously resolved (the female as well as the male members voting) that Mr M should be invited, without delay, to accept the co-pastorship.

148. January 1840, *SMB*.

149. January 9, 1840, *SMB*.

150. January 9, 1840, *SMB*.

151. January 14, 1840, *SMB*.

152. April 10, 1840, *SMB*.

153. February 28, 1840, *SMB*.

154. September 4, 1840, *SMB*.

155. April 30, 1841, *SMB*.

156. December 31, 1841, *SMB*.

157. April 29, 1842, *SMB*.

158. September 30, 1842, *SMB*.

159. February 19, 1843, *SMB*.

160. March 9, 1838, Lion Walk Church Book 6, Essex Record Office, D/NC 52/2/1.

161. April 29, 1842, *SMB*.

162. February 28, 1843, *SMB*.

163. March 16, 1843, A.F.J. Brown, *Essex People 1750–1900, from their diaries, memoirs and letters*, Essex Record Office Publications, No. 59, p. 168.

164. May 29, 1843, A.F.J. Brown, *Essex People 1750–1900, from their diaries, memoirs and letters*, Essex Record Office Publications, No. 59, p. 170.

165. June 2, 1843, *SMB*.

166. Records of the Church of Christ meeting in Head-Gate Chapel, Colchester, 1844, Essex Record Office, D/NC 45/2/2, p. 2.

Chapter 11

167. April 2, 1843, *SMB*.

168. May 5, 1843, *SMB*.

169. September 29, 1843, *SMB*.

170. December 1, 1843, *SMB*.

171. July 4, 1828, *SMB*.

172. August 31, 1832, *SMB*.

173. January 1, 1842, *SMB*.

174. April 30, 1841, *SMB*.

175. November 1, 1844, *SMB*.

176. January 3, 1834, *SMB*.

177. Reminiscences of Joseph Blomfield, St Botolphs, Colchester, May 23 1914, *Essex County Telegraph*.

178. *Chelmsford Chronicle*, Friday November 28, 1845.

179. Reminiscences of Joseph Blomfield, St Botolphs, Colchester, May 23 1914, *Essex County Telegraph*.

180. November 29, 1850, *SMB*.

181. January 3, 1851, *SMB*.

182. *Chelmsford Chronicle*, Friday, March 13, 1896.

183. December 4, 1840, *SMB*.

184. August 1, 1845, *SMB*, and *Essex Standard*, Wednesday 01 August 1855.

185. *The Blomfields of Dedham and Colchester*, Published privately by L.C. Sier, 1924, Colchester Library.

186. *The Blomfields of Dedham and Colchester*, Published privately by L.C. Sier, 1924, Colchester Library.

187. Courtesy Tina Salmon, photographed 11/08/2016, transcribed later.

188. September 3, 1841, *SMB*.

189. October 31, 1856, *SMB*.

Chapter 12

190. Preface to J. Herrick, *Immanuel*.

191. End of letter 5, on Deuteronomy, J. Herrick, *Immanuel*.

192. Beginning of letter 19 on Matthew, J. Herrick, *Immanuel*.

193. Beginning of letter 19 on Matthew, J. Herrick, *Immanuel*.

194. End of letter 20 on Mark and Luke, J. Herrick, *Immanuel*.

195. End of letter 22 on Acts, J. Herrick, *Immanuel*.

196. Introduction, J. Herrick *The Monitory Mirror*, (Religious Tract Society, 1836), p. 1.

197. J. Herrick, *The Monitory Mirror*, pp. 8, 13, 20, 24, 28, 30.

198. J. Herrick, *The Monitory Mirror*, pp. 109–111.

199. J. Herrick, *The greatness of God's mercy in Christ, or salvation possible to the vilest sinners* (London: Simpkin, Marshall, and Co. Ipswich: Burton. Colchester: Harvey, 1842), p. 1.

200. J. Herrick, *The greatness of God's mercy in Christ, or salvation possible to the vilest sinners* (London: Simpkin, Marshall, and Co. Ipswich: Burton. Colchester: Harvey, 1842), p. 2.

201. J. Herrick, *The greatness of God's mercy in Christ, or salvation possible to the vilest sinners* (London: Simpkin, Marshall, and Co. Ipswich: Burton. Colchester: Harvey. 1842), pp. 90–91.

202. J. Herrick, *Salvation certain and complete; or the greatest sinners capable of being rendered holy and happy* (London: Simpkin, Marshall, and Co., Ipswich: Burton, 1845), pp. 26–27.

203. J. Herrick, *Salvation certain and complete; or the greatest sinners capable of being rendered holy and happy* (London: Simpkin, Marshall, and Co., Ipswich: Burton, 1845), pp. 30–31.

204. J. Herrick, *Salvation certain and complete; or the greatest sinners capable of being rendered holy and happy* (London: Simpkin, Marshall, and Co., Ipswich: Burton, 1845), pp. 189–190.

Chapter 13

205. August 1, 1862, *SMB*.

206. Reminiscences of Joseph Blomfield, St Botolphs Colchester, *Essex County Telegraph*, May 1914.

207. From J. Herrick, *Poetic and Prosaic Sketches*.

208. This section adapted and corrected from obituary and funeral notices in *Essex Standard*, Wednesday, 1 February 1865, and *Chelmsford Chronicle*, Friday 10 February 1865.

Chapter 14

209. *Essex Standard,* Friday 10 February 1865, From a Correspondent formerly resident in Colchester.

210. *Essex Standard,* Friday 10 February 1865, From a Correspondent formerly resident in Colchester.

211. Herrick Obituary, *Congregational Year Book* 1866, pp. 260–261.

212. Herrick Obituary, *Congregational Year Book* 1866, pp. 260–261.

213. 'Reminiscences of Joseph Blomfield, St Botolphs, Colchester', May 23, 1914, *Essex County Telegraph*.

214. 'A Copy of an Address from Mr Fry to the Church of Christ at Billericay', September 5, 1798, Essex Record Office, D/NC 25/1.

215. *Essex Standard,* Friday 10 February 1865, From a Correspondent formerly r in Colchester.

216. *Chelmsford Chronicle*, Friday, 9 February 1866.